REVELATIONS
TRAINING MANUAL

Books by Dr. Joe Ibojie

Bible-Based Dictionary of Prophetic Symbols for Every Christian

The Watchman

Dreams and Visions Volume 1—International Best Seller

Dreams and Visions Volume 2

The Justice of God: Victory in Everyday Living

How to Live the Supernatural Life in the Here and Now—International Best Seller

Illustrated Bible-Based Dictionary of Dream Symbols—International Best Seller

Destined for the Top

Times of Refreshing Volume 1

Times of Refreshing Volume 2—New

Revelations Training Manual—New

Available from Cross House Books

REVELATIONS
TRAINING MANUAL
Understanding Your Revelations from God

DR. JOE IBOJIE

 Take note that the name satan and related names are not capitalized. I choose not to acknowledge him, even to the point of violating grammatical rules.

CROSS HOUSE BOOKS
Christian Book Publishers
245 Midstocket Road
Aberdeen
AB15 5PH, UK

"The entrance of Your word brings light."

ISBN: 978-0-9574782-4-4

For Worldwide Distribution, Printed in the U.S.A.

1 2 3 4 5 6 7 8 / 17 16 15 14 13

To order products by Dr. Joe Ibojie and other Cross House Books,

contact sales@crosshousebooks.co.uk.

Other correspondence: info@crosshousebooks.co.uk

Visit: www.crosshousebooks.co.uk

Contents

Introduction

Revelations Training Manual—Understanding Your Revelations from God is a comprehensive, interactive training manual based on my best-selling books. With so many Holy Spirit-inspired experiences gathered over many years of walking with the Lord, I decided that this personal tool would be the perfect complement to these books—allowing you to glean as much wisdom as possible from what God has shared with me.

Suitable for individual use, group study, or as Sunday school discussions, *Revelations Training Manual—Understanding Your Revelations from God* will strengthen your relationship with God, your family, and church community.

A taste of what is presented within the following pages includes:

- How to understand dreams and revelations that prompt and enhance additional releases from Heaven.
- Revelation is God's prerogative; He decides when, where, who, and what to reveal—and you need to know how to recognize His presence.
- God wants to reveal to you His divine will on earth as it is in Heaven.
- It is the Lord's desire for none to perish—that *all* would come to know Him through the revelations He offers.
- How to present a yielded heart to God that encourages more dreams and revelations.

- Intimacy with God sets the stage for revelations.

This manual is designed to help you uncover the beauty of God's love and His deep desire to communicate with you through His revelations. As you take time to consider the insights, questions, and points to ponder, your perspective will be enlightened, your worldview enlarged, and your relationship with your heavenly Father enriched.

PART I

DREAMS AND VISIONS: A PRACTICAL APPROACH

CHAPTER 1

The Handwriting of God

Revealing Revelation

POINTS TO NOTE

1. Experiencing dreams and visions is natural. In fact, they are part of your journey on earth. They are valuable survival tools in a world constantly distancing itself from God. I believe that dreaming is one sure way of receiving fresh mandate from Him. You need to hear God for yourself at a personal level.
2. ***Revelation*** is a result of intimacy with God. Revelatory "gifting" is the potential, or capability, to receive revelation from God. As Psalm 25:14 says, *"The Lord confides in those who fear Him; He makes His covenant known to them."*
3. Only the Holy Spirit gives you a true and correct interpretation of dreams, visions, and mysteries of God. The true meaning of the parables, dreams, mysteries, and "the handwriting of God" are divinely "sealed"; therefore, magicians, enchanters, astrologers, and psychics cannot interpret or understand these revelations—only God.

EXERCISES

A. In what ways have you noticed the world distancing itself from God? Are you guilty of taking this action? If yes, what steps can you take to regain intimacy with God?

Discussion

B. What is the first thing that comes to your mind when you see the word *revelation?* How does it relate to your everyday life?

Discussion

C. What part does the Holy Spirit play in helping you interpret your dreams, visions, and mysteries of God?

Discussion

Dreams from God

POINTS TO NOTE

1. True dreams come from God in the form of a parable language or illustrated stories—they are personalized encoded messages full of symbols expressing the mysteries of God. Because of the symbolism, dreams need interpretation for a proper understanding. Interpretation can come to the dreamer either spontaneously, after praying to God about the dream, or through a believer gifted in dream interpretation.
2. Many hesitate to discover the meaning of their dreams—even though it is biblical to do so. Dream interpretation should be a carefully guided effort because wrong interpretation can lead to bondage.
3. God uses *unique-to-you language* when communicating with you in dreams. He uses *your life experiences, specific personal traits, and biblical examples*. God also uses events in your life that no one knows about except Him. Therefore, a person gifted in dream interpretation can help with understanding, but correct interpretation must come from the dreamer because of the specific, individual features. Correct meaning always lies covertly deep within the spirit of the dreamer—hence a godly interpreter should never urge a dreamer! Don't push interpretation on people; witness will light up from within the dreamer if interpretation is correct.
4. I believe that God speaks to everyone through dreams in one way or another. However, most people are unable to remember their dreams and therefore don't appreciate their importance. Some claim that they do not dream at all, while others don't know what to do with their many dreams. There is diversity in the gift functionality and the capacity to receive dreams.

EXERCISES

A. Can you recall your dreams? How frequently do you remember your dreams? How much significance do you give to your dreams?

Discussion

B. Does knowing that God uses your uniqueness to communicate with you bring you comfort or caution? Why?

Discussion

C. Do you agree that "God speaks to everyone" through dreams? What do you base your answer upon?

Discussion

Dream Events as Potential Circumstances

POINTS TO NOTE

1. God gives you dreams so you can respond appropriately on earth to what He is doing in Heaven. The most important response to a dream is to *pray* for all its elements, events, and persons (both friends and perceived enemies). Pray even before gaining an understanding of the dream's meaning. Next, *record* the dream and *pay attention* to what God might be saying to you—whether a warning, encouragement, or correction.
2. Misunderstandings or fears evoked by a dream are because the dreamer fails to realize that the dream events are *potential* circumstances—they are not inevitable. A dream that warns of danger is so you can avert the danger; a dream with good promises needs to be prayed through to reap the results.
3. Read; Amos 7: 1-3 & Daniel 4:24-37.

EXERCISES

A. "God gives you dreams so you can respond appropriately on earth to what He is doing in Heaven." In your own words, what does this mean?

Discussion

B. Joseph married Mary in response to a dream he had. He moved to Egypt with Mary and the child Jesus when the child's life was in peril.

Discussion

C. Is prayer your first response to a dream? If not, start today.

Discussion

D. Without peace, quietness, and prayers—sentimentality and clouded judgment often result.

Discussion

E. Do you record your dreams? Does recording your dreams make them seem more real or cause another reaction?

Discussion

POINTS TO NOTE

1. God also sends dreams and visions to ultimately align you with His plans—to lead you further into Christ. The purpose of dreams and visions is to break through your rational thought patterns to show you what more God has for you spiritually to hear and believe. Read: Acts 16:6-10; Daniel 4:24-27.
2. There must be a willingness to obey what God says to you in dreams and visions so you can realize His overall end-time purposes. Some dreams have affected the entire destiny of humankind. Therefore, you should consider the relevance of your dreams beyond your immediate personal circumstances.
3. True *dreams* sent by God come in multimedia packages—a mixture of images, metaphors, similes, poems, dreams, and story lines during sleep. Dreams are received in the spirit and then translated into the mind for comprehension. Sanctifying your mind prepares it to receive dreams from your spirit without corruption, despite the background noise of world events.
4. A *vision* is the visual perception of revelation or supernatural occurrence through your spiritual eyes. Visions are often more real and more literal than dreams. You can receive a vision even when your mind is awake.

EXERCISES

A. How aligned are you with God's plans? Would being more attune to your dreams help you get on track with your God-given destiny?

Discussion

B. Do you believe that your dreams have the potential to affect the entire destiny of humankind? Jesus' visionary transfiguration prepared Him for what He was about to suffer. Read Genesis 15:12-13 and Daniel 7:1 and then reconsider your answer.

Discussion

C. Have you experienced a vision? How was it different from your dreams? Read Acts 22:6-9-11; Numbers 12:6.

Discussion

The Message of a Revelation

POINTS TO NOTE

1. The message of a dream or vision can come in many ways or any gift of the Spirit can be imparted in a dream or vision: as prophecy (most common); a word of knowledge; a gift or discernment; a gift of healing; a gift of wisdom; or as a gift of interpretation. Solomon was given wisdom in a dream. God can radically rewrite your life through the dreams you receive.
2. Dreams have the power to expand, confirm, enlighten, enrich, and deepen your understanding of God's Word:

- Dreams give you details and specific direction and such wisdom keys are often embedded in the dream's symbolism. Dreams can also give hidden insight to the situation.
- God does not send dreams to embarrass, condemn, or confuse you.
- In dreams God can grant you insightful understanding of your heart.

3. In modern terms, some dreams or visions may sound like "pizza dreams" that supposedly come from eating junk food too late at night. But in reality most dreams are divinely inspired.

EXERCISES

A. Would you recognize a dream or vision's message that came in the form of a prophecy? A gift of healing or wisdom? Why or why not?

Discussion

B. Are you open to receiving dreams and visions that may radically rewrite the next portion of your life?

Discussion

C. Isaiah was called in a vision, which radically rewrote the next portion of his ministry.

Discussion (See Isaiah 6)

D. How many visions from God have you attributed to "pizza dreams"?

Discussion

The Eyes of Your Heart

POINTS TO NOTE

1. Because you see dreams with the eyes of your heart, *you should not switch off the light in your heart*. God is the light of your heart—if you fill your heart with God, then light will shine in. Commit the last moment of each day to meditating on God's Word and preparing your heart's spiritual soil for whatever dreams God may give you.
2. Record your nightly encounters with God. Keep a pen and notebook or tape recorder nearby. Meditate on the meaning of your dreams after you have recorded them, capturing the essence of what God is saying to you (see Prov. 25:2).
3. Fasting and prayer heighten sensitivity to the Spirit. Fasting allows you to receive revelation faster and at a deeper level. Receiving clear revelation is somehow connected to the purity of your lifestyle and obedience to God. Adding God's Word to your fasting releases faith, which is your "eye" for operating in the supernatural. Consider Peter's fasting and prayers:

   > *About noon the following day as they were on their journey and approaching the city, Peter went up on the roof **to pray**. He became hungry and wanted something to eat, and while the meal was being prepared, he fell into a trance* (Acts 10:9-10).

EXERCISES

A. What does seeing dreams with the eyes of your heart mean to you? Have you had this experience?

Discussion

____

____

____

B. How serious are you about fasting? What is your attitude about fasting?

Discussion

____

____

____

C. Do you "operate in the supernatural"? Do you use your spiritual senses?

Discussion

D. Before falling asleep each night, do you meditate on God's goodness and kindness?

Discussion

Remembering Your Dreams

POINTS TO NOTE

1. A dream and its vital details may also be lost if you are not at peace; therefore, you need quiet time to recall your dreams. Before a day's busyness starts, allow time for dreams to drift into the image center of your mind.
2. Remembering dreams can be hindered by the effects of alcohol, bitterness, anger, resentment, medication, and even physical exhaustion. Also, trying to interpret a dream before its full recollection and recording causes the loss of vital parts of a dream. Recall your dreams immediately upon awaking; just as the prophet Zechariah did (see Zech. 4:1-2).
3. Dreams actually line up in your spirit, wait for your mind to wake up, and then get translated in the first few minutes of your being awake. However some dreamers may sometimes think their way through things while dreaming. Dreams are written in spiritual ink that quickly fades; you must transcribe them into durable ink of your memory. Write down what you receive, whether it is clear or not (see Dan. 7:1).

EXERCISES

A. Do you remember all your dreams? Some of your dreams? Only a few of your dreams?

Discussion

B. Will you make time each morning to write down the dreams you have had?

Discussion

C. Why is it important to know what God is revealing to you through your dreams?

Discussion

Recording Your Dreams

POINTS TO NOTE

4. A dream is often like one scene in a movie, which makes it important to record all your dreams to build up a broad picture. Review your dream recordings to gain a wider perspective of what God is saying. You might discover a missing element that makes the message complete (see 1 Chron. 28:19).
5. Recording your dreams often reveals details that might have been lost. Revelation should always be recorded for several important reasons:

- Future circumstances may suggest that you have misheard God.
- You can confront your circumstances with hopeful expectation of your revelation, as opposed to letting your natural circumstances seemingly deny it.
- Recorded revelation is not easily forgotten amid the storms of life.
- Recorded revelations can be reviewed by others.

EXERCISES

A. Have you received portions of dreams that later fit together to form a complete scenario?

Discussion

B. Do you routinely write down: what to buy at the grocery store, the date and time of your next dentist appointment, how many cookies to make for the bake sale, how many board members will be attending the next meeting, etc.? If yes, then make it a practice to write the essence of your dreams and visions, as well.

Discussion

C. How good is your memory? If you are like most people, recording important events is critical to remembering details. Start tomorrow morning.

Discussion

___

___

___

The Difference Between Revelations

POINTS TO NOTE

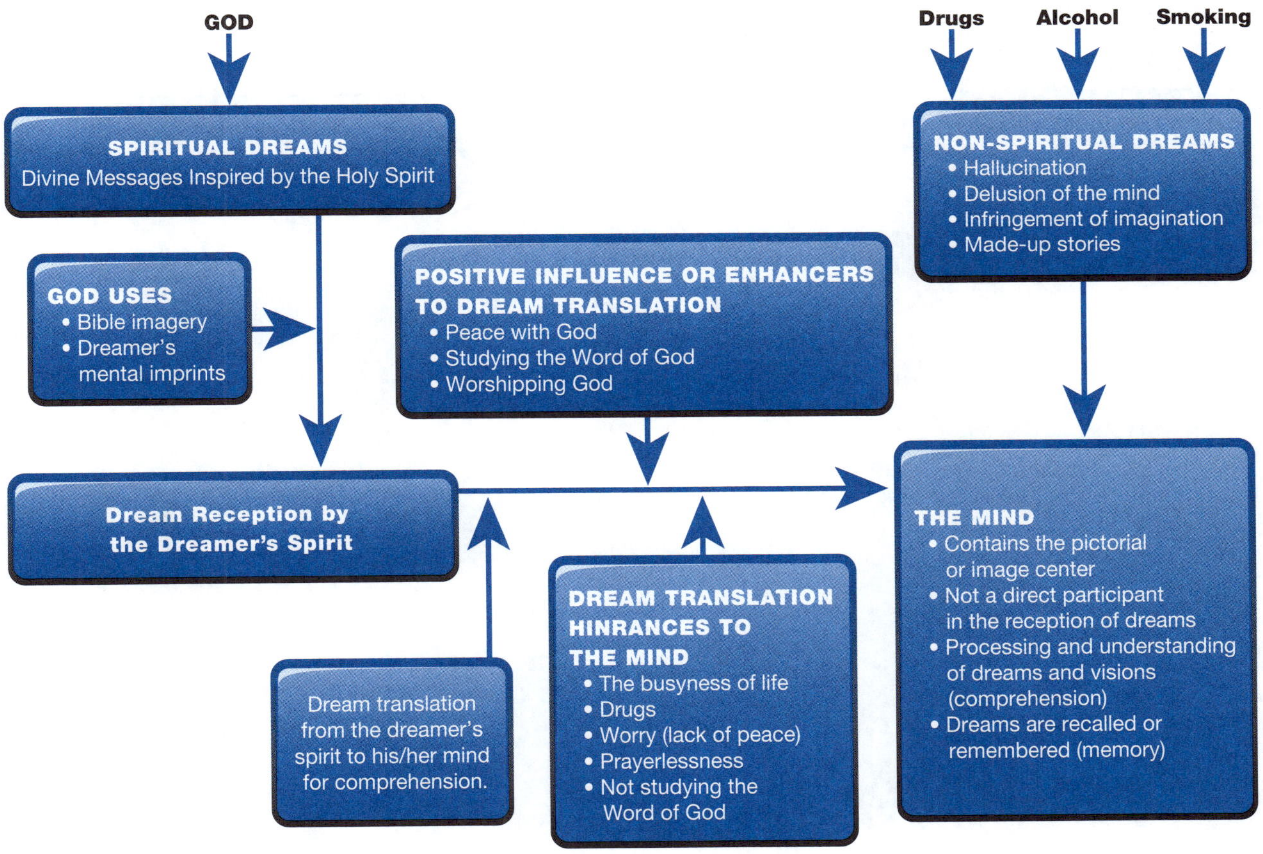

EXERCISES

A. What other non-spiritual influences and their consequences can you name?

Discussion

B. Name three more positive influences or enhancers to dream translations.

Discussion

C. Name three more hindrances to dream translations.

Discussion

PRACTICAL PRINCIPLES AND DISCUSSION

CHAPTER 2

How to Receive Dreams and Visions

POINTS TO NOTE

4. God releases dreams and visions to your spirit. The impartation is enhanced by the state of your spirit determined by factors such as: spiritual wisdom, a sanctified conscience, and communion with God.
   - **Spiritual wisdom** is the practical application of the Word of God that always comes from Heaven. (See James 3:17.) *Wisdom is comprehensive insight into the ways and purposes of God, as revealed in His Word.*
   - **A sanctified conscience** is one washed by the blood of Jesus, *transcending the limits of the intellect.* It operates by laying down personal agendas and preferring the interest of others to your own.
   - **Communion with God** is the basis on which wisdom and conscience are birthed and maintained in God. Constant communion between your spirit and the Spirit of God enhances the planting (engaging with the meaning) of dreams in your spirit.
5. Being submitted to God also enhances automatic sowing of dreams into your spirit. This factor is pivotal: *"How much more should we* ***submit to the Father of*** **[our]** ***spirits and live!"*** (Heb. 12:9b).

EXERCISES

A. Do you believe your spirit is open to receiving God's dreams and visions?

Discussion

B. What is the state of your spiritual wisdom? Do you have a sanctified conscience? How well are you communicating with God?

Discussion

C. How submitted to God are you? Is there room for improvement?

Discussion

Spirit, Mind, Capacity

POINTS TO NOTE

1. **The role of your mind.** Your *spirit* receives the dream or revelation, your *mind* receives information—the prophetic is received in the spirit. The link between your spirit and your mind is *faith*. The mind puts things together, though it can not understand revelation. Dreams and revelations may not seem logical to your mind. Your mind wants to be in control, but the spirit is gentle and wants to commune and move with God. *Peace, quietness, and rest are prerequisites* for the mind to relate to the spirit and to make the revelation relevant to the dreamer's circumstance.

2. Your **capacity to receive dreams** is a gift—*a special ability*. It is important to realize that:

   - A gift is *not a reward*—you do not earn it.
   - Giftedness is *not* necessarily *a sign of maturity*.
   - This gift is *not* equivalent to *good character*.
   - It does *not validate* your walk with God.
   - You can have a spiritual gift and *not know it*.
   - A spiritual gift can be *dormant* or *active*.
   - A spiritual gift can *run* in a family

3. **A spiritual gift has a dual existence:** it exists in the spirit realm and the natural realm. There is full expression when it exists in the *spirit* and *natural* realms. A spiritual gift can skip a generation by not manifesting in the natural, but it always exists in heavenly places because it is irrevocable: *"The gifts and calling of God are irrevocable"* (Rom. 11:29). The outworking in the natural can be enhanced or frustrated or cursed!

EXERCISES

A. Knowing that your *spirit* receives the dream or revelation and your *mind* receives information, how much more powerful is your spirit over your mind? Is your faith link between your spirit and your mind as strong as it should be?

Discussion

____

____

____

B. Do you have the gift to receive dreams and revelations? Why or why not?

Discussion

____

____

____

C. Have you witnessed the outworking of this gift in the spirit *and* the natural realm?

Discussion

____

____

____

Hindrances to Receiving Dreams

POINTS TO NOTE

Consider these ways that you may be hindering revelations from God after reading First Samuel 3:1-2; Amos 8:11-12; Deuteronomy 28:15,23.

1. God's ultimate objective of communicating through dreams is to call the dreamer to action. If action is not taken, the value and purpose of the dream is unrealized, and God may withhold additional dreams and visions. (See Appendix A.)
2. If there is no peace in your spirit, dreams are hindered. Your spirit must be in a condition to release to the mind and receive what God is giving. You must live in the peace of God, and maintain the unity of the Spirit through the bond of peace.

3. When you grieve the Holy Spirit, the Holy Spirit withdraws from you, and you do not receive revelation (see Eph. 4:29-32).
4. The planting of dreams and visions is hindered when you go to bed angry (see Eph. 4:26-27).
5. God does not give revelation if you are prideful. God resists the proud and exalts the humble. He may protect you from becoming too proud by sealing parts of dreams.
6. Alcohol and drugs can depress reception and remembrance of dreams. Drugs and chemicals cannot cause you to have dreams. But they do produce hallucinations, which are quite different from true dreams. Blurred images and distorted, fragmented dreams can result from planting dreams in your soul rather than in your spirit.

EXERCISES

A. Think of a few ways that you may be hindering dream reception.

Discussion

___

___

___

B. Think of a few ways you can open yourself to receiving more dreams from God.

Discussion

___

___

___

C. Have you experienced the difference between Spirit-inspired dreams and those that were chemically induced? How were they different?

Discussion

___

___

___

The Evil Revelatory Delay

POINTS TO NOTE

Consider these ways that the devil may be hindering your revelations from God:

1. Satan can withhold your revelations in the heavenly: Then he continued, *"Do not be afraid, Daniel. Since the first day that you set your mind to gain understanding and to humble yourself before your God, your words were heard, and I have come in response to them. But the prince of the Persian kingdom resisted me twenty-one days. Then Michael, one of the chief princes, came to help me, because I was detained there with the king of Persia. Now I have come to explain to you what will happen to your people in the future, for the vision concerns a time yet to come"* (Daniel 10:12-14).

   - He inputs information into your mind so it appears as revelation to cause confusion and deception.
   - He hinders a dreamer's ability to translate what the spirit receives. Blocking a translation is a major way the devil hinders the remembrance of dreams. Visions are less affected this way.

2. When the work of satan is responsible for poor reception and remembrance of dreams, it is usually characterized by:

   - Frustration
   - Anxiety
   - Lack of peace
   - Insecurity
   - A feeling of emptiness

3. During this time of delay when reception is hindered and translation of spiritual experience to your memory is hindered, God will often give revelation through other means.

EXERCISES

A. Has satan incessantly intruded into your mind to the point where you were unable to focus on God and His love for you? What did you do to counteract satan's tactics?

Discussion

B. Do you think your dreams have been hindered by satan's interjection of frustration, anxiety, lack of peace, insecurity, or feelings of emptiness? Trusting and submitting to God is the answer.

Discussion

C. Have you received revelation from God through other means?

Discussion

How Visions are Received

POINTS TO NOTE

1. You can receive a vision with your natural eyes wide open but see the vision in the spirit. In apparitions, the supernatural happenings can be perceived with the natural senses and even experienced tangibly.
2. Visions are spiritual encounters with differing points of involvement in the physical realm. In Genesis, Jacob had a visionary encounter with an angel that left him with a physical deformity (see Gen. 32:24-25). Unlike dreams—in which encounters are on a purely individual basis—visions can be corporate because of their involvement in the natural realm, though individual perception of the same encounter may vary.
3. Paul described a visionary experience in which he was not sure whether or not he was in the body (see 2 Cor. 12:2).

EXERCISES

A. Have you had a vision? What made it different from dreams you have had?

Discussion

B. How is seeing in the spirit different from seeing in the natural? If you haven't experienced this, imagine the difference.

Discussion

C. Have you ever experienced a similar version as Paul describes in Second Corinthians 12:2? How did it make you feel?

Discussion

Keys to "Open Heaven" Activation

POINTS TO NOTE

1. A temporary opening of a "third heaven" over your head—*"And your heavens which are over your head..."* (Deut. 28:23 NKJV)—may be facilitated by you doing the following:

- Exercise your spiritual senses on a constant basis (see Heb. 5:14 NKJV).
- Ensure that every experience in your spiritual life is Bible-guided. Exercise the practice of waiting upon God to activate the seer anointing.
- Strengthen your spirit (see Eph. 1:16-18).
- Ensure that you see with eyes of faith. Sanctify your imagination. Position yourself where God can initiate a spiritual experience. Keep your heart and motives pure. Control your mind and learn to quiet your soul before the Lord. Be careful what you hear or see; it all affects your spiritual senses and spiritual experiences.
- Apply the blood of the Lamb (see Heb. 9:12).
- Pray and fast (see 2 Chron. 7:14; 1 Kings 3:4-5).
- Give tithes and offerings (see Acts 10:2-4; Mal. 3:10).
- Meditate on the Word of God (see 2 Pet. 1:19; Rom. 8:11).

EXERCISES

A. How familiar are you with the "open heaven" concept? What do these terms mean to you?

Discussion

B. How many of the eight actions mentioned are you currently doing: on a regular basis, frequently, infrequently?

Discussion

C. Have you learned how to control your mind and quiet your soul before the Lord? How easy was this for you to learn? Are you still learning?

Discussion

High, Medium, and Low Volume Dreamers

POINTS TO NOTE

1. What is received and how it is received depends on your relationship with God. Some people are gifted to receive variable volumes of revelations. The essential point is how dreamers put giftedness to use. God meets each dreamer's needs within his or her level of giftedness.
2. There are high, medium, and low volume dreamers:
   - *High volume* dreamers receive as many as two or more dreams in a single night on a consistent basis. The majority of what a high volume dreamer receives may address issues pertaining to routines of life that most people would not imagine God to be interested in.

- *Medium volume* dreamers receive an amount in-between the other two categories.
- *Low volume* dreamers receive about one dream a week or one dream in a few weeks, on a fairly regular basis.
- *Others, or so-called non-dreamers,* include those who claim to be non-dreamers because they cannot recall their dreams.

3. Most dreamers operate below their gifted potential; therefore, there is always room for advancement when you pay attention to dreams and move closer to God. It is possible to increase the scope of your dreams' coverage to include non-personal issues.
4. As you mature in Christ, you communicate more closely with God and get sharper, clearer, and shorter dreams. Multiple dreams in one night may refer to different aspects of a message or different scenes of the same story; this is common in the life of high volume dreamers.

EXERCISES

A. Do you consider yourself a high, medium, or low volume dreamer?

Discussion

B. Do you agree that when you were first born again you received more lengthy dreams?

Discussion

C. Do you aspire to be a high volume dreamer? What steps can you take to reach your goal?

Discussion

PRACTICAL PRINCIPLES AND DISCUSSION

CHAPTER 3

Seeking Meaning

POINTS TO NOTE

1. It is biblical to seek understanding of a dream or vision. Many believe that since the Holy Spirit gives dream interpretations that they do not need to search for meaning themselves. However, the Bible says, *"It is the glory of God to conceal a matter; to search out a matter is the glory of kings"* (Prov. 25:2).
2. Like Gideon, the Lord can use *other people* to give you interpretation of *your* dreams in much the same way as *you* can give interpretations for others' dreams by giving exposition of Scripture, even though the Holy Spirit is your teacher. It's important to build up a dictionary of dream symbols that God uses to communicate with you.
3. Every dream comes with *an inbuilt drive* to search for the true meaning. This divine drive can last for years, fading only when true interpretation has been found. This inbuilt drive reflects the divine premium placed on such a dream according to the degree of divine premium placed on it by God. You cannot talk a dreamer out of looking for the true meaning of a dream with high divine premium and inbuilt drive! This inbuilt drive only fades when correct interpretation is received.
4. Many people ask, "Why would a loving God speak to His children in 'obscure language,' which is difficult to understand because of its symbolism?" This question is reminiscent of what the disciples asked our Lord Jesus Christ during His earthly ministry (see Matt. 13:10-13 AMP).

EXERCISES

A. Has someone else ever interpreted correctly a dream or vision of yours?

Discussion

B. Have you ever interpreted correctly a dream or vision of another person?

Discussion

C. Why do you think God chooses to communicate at times through an obscure language?

Discussion

Gaining Spiritual Knowledge and Wisdom

POINTS TO NOTE

1. When you seek a dream's meaning, you gain spiritual knowledge and wisdom. What is revealed is for your benefit, but a dream's benefits are not yours until its meaning is revealed (see Deut. 29:29). If you do not pursue the dream's meaning, the revelation may not benefit you.
2. Your dreams create a desire for understanding, no matter what circumstances you are in or where you are geographically (see Gen. 40:6-8).
3. God reigns supreme, be it in a palace or prison dungeon. The king of the then most powerful state on earth needed answers to questions raised by his dreams (see Gen. 41:8,14-16).
4. King Nebuchadnezzar of Babylon also sought meaning of his dreams on four different occasions (see Daniel 2:1-3,16; 4:18).
5. King Belshazzar, ruler of Babylon, also sought interpretation of a puzzle or divine riddle (see Dan. 5:5,16).

EXERCISES

A. Does knowing that powerful and important biblical people sought the meaning of their dreams make you feel more comfortable wanting to know the meaning of yours?

Discussion

B. In all honesty, what would be your reaction to seeing *"the fingers of a human hand appeared and wrote on the plaster of the wall"*?

Discussion

C. Are you afraid of a similar "scary" event happening if you seek out your dreams' meanings?

Discussion

Confirmation of Interpretation

POINTS TO NOTE

1. God can confirm interpretation in many different ways, including hearing God's audible voice or through an inner voice, other dreams and visions, and even mental pictures to inner impressions. You can become more receptive to His voice and more attentive to His ways through prayer, fasting, meditation, worship, and studying Scripture.

2. Confirmation through prophets, other forms of prophecy, events (past or ongoing), and God's other revelatory means, including recurring dreams is also possible. *Avoid* the following when confirming whether a dream interpretation is correct:

- The danger of over-spiritualizing. Be alert and wait upon the Holy Spirit to quicken you about what is important.
- The danger of becoming too "sign dependent." To demand a sign at every stage is to doubt God or lack boldness to act on your belief. The Bible tells us that faith without works is dead (see James 2:17). Gideon was too sign-dependent (see Judg. 6:17,36-40).
- Failing to act on your dream for lack of details. The fullness of a dream will unfold with time as you obey and let the Lord lead you.

EXERCISES

A. In what ways are you listening for God to confirm His plans in your life?

Discussion

B. Are you sometimes guilty of being sign-dependent?

Discussion

C. Do you become impatient when waiting for God to confirm the interpretation of a dream?

Discussion

Help From the Holy Spirit

POINTS TO NOTE

1. With the Holy Spirit's help, you can interact with God in a dream and handle what is received. A true dream is the divinely coded parable language of God. Without the Holy Spirit, you cannot understand this language, even if it appears to be simple. (See Genesis 41:7-8 and First Corinthians 2:13-14.)
2. True dreams, parables of God, reflect the ways of God; they transcend the limits of human understanding. Jesus' disciples asked Him for explanations, and He explained meanings to them in private. He also promised that the Holy Spirit would help them understand (see John 14:25-26).

EXERCISES

A. Are you filled with the Holy Spirit?

Discussion

B. The Holy Spirit is your comforter and counselor. In what ways has the Holy Spirit shown Himself to you on a regular basis?

Discussion

C. Do other Scripture passages come to mind as you consider these truths? How possible is it that the Holy Spirit has brought these words to your heart?

Discussion

Interpretation by the Holy Spirit

POINTS TO NOTE

In my experience, the Holy Spirit can enable you to interpret a dream in three ways:

1. *A word of knowledge regarding God's mind in sending the dream.* A majority of Christians can gain insight into their dreams by a word of knowledge. God commonly answers when you ask Him for the meaning of your dreams. This is how God sows relevant scriptural passages in the dreamer after a dream to point to the dream's meaning. In the Scriptures, most angelic interpretations to a dreamer's prayers came as a word of knowledge. This is also how some people with an established prophetic ministry gain understanding of dreams (shortcut but usually accurate!).
2. *The gift of interpretation.* The gift of interpretation is an offshoot of the gift of wisdom from the Holy Spirit; it is a sovereign gift from the Lord.
3. *Acquiring interpretative skills.* Every dreamer needs interpretative skills in addition to the preceding two gifts. Interpretation is made sharper by practice. It is a great resource in gaining understanding of dreams. Whether gifted in interpretation or not, you need to be able to appropriately explain the relevance of symbols in a dreamer's life. This often comes by acquiring interpretative skills.

EXERCISES

A. What does the term "word of knowledge" mean to you? Have you ever received a word of knowledge either for yourself or others?

Discussion

B. Have you identified your gifts from the Holy Spirit? Are you sharing them with others?

Discussion

C. How prepared are you to expound on the relevance of symbols?

Discussion

Hidden Meaning in Dreams and Visions

POINTS TO NOTE

1. The hidden things of God are beyond human understanding by natural reasoning; they are purposely sealed by the Holy Spirit until a set time. Every dreamer will have many of these hidden things in dreams. Unless the Lord reveals their meaning, they remain obscured.
2. A "Daniel-type anointing" is the ability to understand all types of dreams and visions in which God releases meaning. A "Daniel-type anointing" requires a person to have the humility needed to recognize when a hidden meaning exists and to ask God for its understanding. This dependency helps keep the gifted interpreter in humble submission to the Holy Spirit.
3. An angel revealed a hidden meaning to Daniel (see Dan. 8:15-25). In other instances, Daniel acknowledged that only God knows what has been hidden in the dark (see Dan. 2:19-22 and 12:8-10). The Bible says Daniel had understanding of all types of dreams (see Dan. 1:17) because he had the humility to seek meaning of the hidden things not yet revealed to him.
4. The first step in gaining understanding of the hidden meaning of dreams is to have a desire to gain understanding, and then ask God to reveal it (see Dan. 7:15-16).

EXERCISES

A. How easy is it to praise and worship God when you think He may be holding back a revelation from you?

Discussion

B. Knowing something that someone else wants to know can produce pride and arrogance. How did Daniel resist the temptation of an inflated ego?

Discussion

C. What steps can you take to keep from becoming prideful?

Discussion

PRACTICAL PRINCIPLES AND DISCUSSION

CHAPTER 4

Hearing God's Voice

POINTS TO NOTE

1. It is important that you hear the voice of God. *Hearing God's voice is not an option*—it is a necessity of a healthy spiritual life. It's an indispensible survival tool to navigate the intrigues of life. Many perish because they cannot hear God's voice, and are unable to usher His counsel into the realities of their lives.
2. Job was a righteous man of outstanding reputation; nevertheless, Job suffered and he failed to hear the voice of God on a personal level. Job was rightly focused on the circumstances of his natural existence, and he suffered consequences from a lack of prophetic insight.
3. You are called to a prophetic lifestyle and to live the supernatural in your life. I believe that the wishes of Moses are being fulfilled in this generation (see Num. 11:29). Seize the momentum and be part of this glorious fulfillment.

EXERCISES

A. Do you know God on a personal level? Do you have a personal relationship with Him?

Discussion

B. How would you define your relationship with the Triune God? Intimate, personal, casual, other?

Discussion

C. Why do you think Job didn't hear God on a personal level? Be specific.

Discussion

The Logos and Rhema Word of God

POINTS TO NOTE

1. The *logos* Word (the written Bible) is what God says to everyone. What He says to an individual on a personal level is the *rhema* word of God. *"In the past God spoke to our ancestors through the prophets at many times and in various ways, but in these last days he has spoken to us by his Son"* (Heb. 1:1-2a). Jesus Christ is the Word of God.
2. A *rhema* word is an inspired word of God birthed within your own spirit, like the still small voice that spoke to Elijah in the cave (see 1 Kings 19). The breakthrough strategy for any circumstance is discerning the *rhema* word for that particular situation.

EXERCISES

A. Do you regularly hear God's voice? Why or why not?

Discussion

B. What is the most common way for you to hear God's voice?

Discussion

C. How good are you at discerning the *rhema* word in different situations?

Discussion

Realize the Deep Things of God

POINTS TO NOTE

1. In Luke 5:4, Peter received a breakthrough by heeding a *rhema* word for his life: *"When He* [Christ] *had finished speaking, He said to Simon, 'Put out into deep water, and let down the nets for a catch.'"* Note that after Jesus finished speaking generally, He spoke personally to Peter to launch out into the deep. Peter had the choice whether or not to obey.
2. After laboring all night without success, Peter had every reason not to obey. Many questions must have passed through his mind, as they would for you under similar circumstances.
3. Peter let down the nets and caught an incredibly large number of fish, so much so that the boat almost capsized. Peter's ability to discern what the Lord was saying to him on a personal level resulted in a miraculous catch of fish. From that moment on, he surrendered the frailty of his human mind to the sovereignty and superior wisdom of Almighty God (see Luke 5:8). Peter was later entrusted with the leadership of the early Church.

EXERCISES

A. How closely are you listening for a *rhema* word from God in your life?

Discussion

B. Do you sometimes think you know better than God? How stubborn are you?

Discussion

C. Have you surrendered the frailty of your human mind to God? Totally?

Discussion

Use Your Spiritual Senses

POINTS TO NOTE

1. Many voices exist in the spirit world. Therefore, whatever is heard must be tested: *Does it exalt Jesus Christ? Does it comply with the Scriptures? Does it put the interest of others before self-interest? Does it encourage unity in the Body of Christ? Does it seek peace of all? Does it give hope no matter what it speaks of? Does it have respect for human life? Does it speak of the love of God?* The answers to these questions help you distinguish the voice of God from other voices (see Heb. 5:14 NKJV).

2. Maturity in the spirit only comes through a process of consistently using your spiritual senses. Mature believers, through consistent exercise of their spiritual senses, can discriminate between sound and unsound doctrines and between wholesome and unwholesome conduct.

3. If you are afraid of misunderstanding what God says, you will never master the art of hearing God and walking in His obedience. Approach the issue with reverence and realize that no one prevails except by the strength of the Holy Spirit.

4. Hearing from God begins where you are and then progresses toward maturity. Divine inspiration may occur to you as a mere impression or a prompting, such as a flash of ideas, a picture, a birthing in the spirit, or even a knowing in your conviction.

5. Your only security lies in walking in love and in realizing that you must come to God with transparent innocence and simplicity. Stepping out in faith will move you from the stage of impression into greater spiritual encounters with divinity.

EXERCISES

A. Are you confused by the voices you hear? Will asking the set of questions provided help you to sort out all of the voices?

Discussion

B. How many divine inspirations have you encountered over your lifetime? Are you actively seeking them?

Discussion

C. What does walking in love toward greater spiritual encounters with divinity mean to you?

Discussion

The Human Spirit

POINTS TO NOTE

1. The spirit is the center of humankind; functionally it consists of *communion:* the power derived from dwelling in His presence (see Ps. 16, 91); *conscience:* the ability to discern; innate ability to know wrong or right; that which has been sanctified by the blood of Jesus (see Heb. 9:14); and *wisdom:* life's application of the Word of God (see James 3:17), which is also called wisdom from above.
2. After the Fall, the reality of your Christian walk is that your soul and spirit are pitted against each other in a conflict of warfare (see Gal. 6:17 NKJV). When the soul becomes prominent, the spirit gets diminished and vice versa. When your spirit is strong, then you can correctly hear and discern what God is saying. To strengthen your spirit, you should train and exercise your spirit (see 1 Tim. 4:7-8 TLB).

3. This relationship is like a tug-of-war: *communion* versus *emotion*; *conscience* versus *mind*; and *wisdom* versus *will*. On the whole, a strong spirit enhances the art of hearing God.

EXERCISES

A. After reading Psalms 16 and 91, define communion in your own words.

Discussion

B. After reading Hebrews 9:14, define conscience in your own words.

Discussion

C. After reading James 3:17, define wisdom in your own words.

Discussion

Divine Advancement

POINTS TO NOTE

1. Dreams and visions are valuable tools in the divine advancement in God's kingdom. Evil has multiplied and worldly wisdom has grown. Consequently, there's an emerging need for spiritual matters to be accurate so you can be victorious over today's challenges. These days are like when God heralded Jesus Christ's birth and ministry with a series of short, clear, and directional dreams, visions, and angelic interactions.

2. More than ever before, if God so desires, dreams and visions will keep you in tune with His heart, particularly when other methods have failed.
3. You can equate dreams and visions *as divine, audio-visual, strategic dialogues that have lingering impact on dreamers in ways that words alone cannot*. Visual impact brings a dreamer into a degree of faith that leads to conviction and commitment.
4. The evolving history of dreams over periods recorded in the Bible can be likened to a "dispensational pattern" of dreams and visions when God communicated with humankind according to a particular spiritual closeness, with clarity, interaction, and angelic involvement. During each period, God gave a variable degree of wisdom, grace, and special attributes to dreamers.

EXERCISES

A. How are dreams and visions valuable tools in the advancement of the Kingdom?

Discussion

B. Are you a "visual" person? Do you learn more quickly if you have visual aids? Why is that?

Discussion

C. Have you experienced a spiritual closeness that involved angels?

Discussion

The Days Ahead

POINTS TO NOTE

1. I believe that the coming days will see a return to interactive dreams, dialoguing in dreams, and more trances, translations, and angelic encounters. This will be the time for a fulfillment of the prophecy given by the prophet Joel, which was again reiterated by the apostle Peter (see Acts: 2:17-18).
2. It is my opinion that knowledge of God's glory permeating the air will multiply the number and clarity of dreams and visions. This time will also see a marked increase in an awareness of angelic ministry (see Hab. 2:14). The Spirit of God poured out upon all flesh will result in an increase in dreams in a supernatural atmosphere.
3. God will reawaken the Joseph and Daniel-type anointing (see Dan. 1:17). God will once again bring men and women to this level of great insightful knowledge through the Holy Spirit's help.

EXERCISES

A. What are your feelings about this fulfillment of the prophecy given by the prophet Joel?

Discussion

B. What does *the knowledge of the glory of the Lord* mean to you?

Discussion

C. If God gave you a choice of accepting a Joseph or a Daniel-type anointing, which would you choose? Why?

Discussion

PRACTICAL PRINCIPLES AND DISCUSSION

CHAPTER 5

Dreamland

RTM

POINTS TO NOTE

1. Dreaming is like experiencing the spiritual atmosphere of the Garden of Eden where a dreamer can often do what is humanly impossible or beyond the scope of human imagination. Therefore, I refer to this atmosphere as "dreamland."

2. I call it dreamland because often dreamers may have encounters with the same people, the same place, and further previous discussions in many dreams. I have dreamt of a particular city over a period of many years. At first it was like uncultivated farm land, and as years went by it became transformed into a lively modern city full of people and activities. The city started appearing in my dreams from the time I gave my life to Christ, and the last time I saw the city in my dream was sometime in 2010. That city symbolizes my life transformation to Christ-likeness; *the city is me!* The prophet Ezekiel said, *"Then the cherubim rose upward. These were the living creatures **I had seen by the Kebar River**"* (meaning in an earlier vision) (Ezek. 10:15; compare Ezek. 1).

3. Conceptually, "dreamland" is the land of the spirit; the mind is almost completely closed, and God can take you backward or forward in time. ***God is supreme in dreamland*** (see Col. 1:16).

4. Other characteristics of dreamland:

- Evil exists in dreamland, in spite of the spiritual atmosphere that prevails just as it was in Eden.
- Humankind's understanding transcends the limits of physical intellect.
- People can be imparted to or receive impartation from God.
- Any dream not sent by God is false, a made-up story and a delusion of the human mind.
- If God allows a dreamer to see activities of the evil ones, it is often called a demonic dream. If God allows a dreamer to see the intent and depths of soul, it is often referred to as a soul dream. Other dreams can be classified according to God's purpose for giving them, or by what God allowed to dominate in the dream's dramatization.
- The language of dreamland is the *parable language of the Spirit, which is the use of symbols to dramatize revelation.*

EXERCISES

A. What images and feelings come to your mind and spirit when you hear the word *dreamland?*

Discussion

B. Have you experienced a demonic dream or a soul dream?

Discussion

C. Explain what the "parable language of the Spirit" means to you.

Discussion

Image Center

POINTS TO NOTE

1. Spiritual revelation is fed into the mind from the human spirit. Functionally, the mind consists of:

- **Memory**, a word depository that deals with past issues.
- **Contemplation**, which deals with current issues and conceptualization.
- **Imagination**, which contains the pictorial depository and handles future issues, such as planning and conceptualization.

2. This pictorial depository of your imagination is your mind's image center, which should be conducive to receiving pictorial revelations from the spirit and capable of resisting pollution from unholy, worldly images.
3. The human brain has two sides that respond differently to specific types of stimuli:

- The left hemisphere's forte is analysis, reason, and logic.
- The right hemisphere is dominant in visual and other sensory processes, as well as in exercising emotion and recognizing humor and metaphor.
- Conceptual and emotionally neutral words activate the left hemisphere.
- Words that name images and are emotionally laden activate the right hemisphere.

EXERCISES

A. If spiritual revelation is fed into the mind from the human spirit, how important is it to keep your mind focused on God?

Discussion

B. How can you make your image center more conducive to receive pictorial revelations from the spirit, and be made capable of resisting pollution from unholy, worldly images?

Discussion

C. Which side of the brain do you think you operate from most frequently?

Discussion

Sanctification of Your Imagination

POINTS TO NOTE

1. Your image center needs sanctification on a regular and continuous basis by not using it for evil, unclean images and thoughts. Protecting the image center allows the Holy Spirit to prepare it to more easily receive divine spiritual inspirations, which opens you for more spiritual encounters.
2. The level of your faith and the busyness of your mind influence translation from your spirit to your image center. Dreams translate to your image center more successfully when the mind is still. Spend some quiet time after waking up so that dreams can drift from the spirit into the image center before the day's demands set in.
3. The human mind processes information in pictures. Images in the pictorial depository have a gripping effect on a person and are often hard to erase. As a consequence, addictions such as pornography, or phobias such as the fear of heights, are the most difficult to overcome.

EXERCISES

A. How adept are you at sanctifying your image center?

Discussion

B. Because dreams translate to your image center more successfully when the mind is still, have you made a practice of being still?

Discussion

C. Do you know from experience that addictions such as pornography or phobias are the most difficult to overcome?

Discussion

Sanctification of Your Imagination and Receiving Divine Revelation

POINTS TO NOTE

1. God expresses spiritual truth in spiritual words. Practicing holy imaginations through meditation on Bible images sanctifies the image center (see Ps. 119:27). A conscience effort should be made to override constant bombardment of worldly imagery that pollutes your image center.
2. Sanctify the image center by filling your imagination with images from God's Word and by reading and visualizing the Scriptures. Sanctification leads to the spirit of sound mind (see 2 Tim. 1:7 NKJV). A sound mind is one balanced and anchored in God. The spirit of a sound mind enables you to enter into godly liberty (see 2 Cor. 3:17 NKJV).
3. Revelation can be distorted in an image center that is polluted with unclean and ungodly images. That is why the Bible describes the pure in heart as follows: *"To the pure, all things are pure, but to those who are corrupted and do not believe, nothing is pure. In fact, both their minds and consciences are corrupted"* (Titus 1:15).
4. Purifying your imagination comes from constant practice of visualizing holy imagery in the Scriptures. Worshiping and listening to anointed Christian teaching helps sanctify your mind.

EXERCISES

A. Do you daily make a conscience effort to override the constant bombardment of worldly imagery that pollutes your image center?

Discussion

B. Do you feel liberty in your spirit so you can operate in the supernatural?

Discussion

C. Purifying your imagination comes from constant practice of visualizing holy imagery in the Scriptures. What is the first holy image that comes to your mind when you think of Psalms?

Discussion

Planting Dreams (Engaging with Your Dream's Message)

POINTS TO NOTE

1. If you sow in the spirit, then you will reap in the spirit; if you sow in the soul, then you will reap in the soul. If you plant a good dream promise in the spirit realm, then you will reap the fruit of the Holy Spirit: *"But the fruit of the Spirit is love, joy, peace, forbearance, kindness, goodness, faithfulness"* (Gal. 5:22).
2. On the other hand, planting a dream in the *soul* realm can *result in anxiety, worry, anger, bitterness, vengeance, unholy fear, hopelessness, condemnations, and insecurity*. Planting your dream in the soul realm is when your emotions and mindsets cloud your understanding; you become blind to the dream's real spiritual connotations and therefore its message.
3. The result of planting a dream in the *spirit* includes peace, love, and self-control, faith in God, drawing closer to God, and trusting that all is well. You truthfully accept when God guides you over circumstances, even if it runs contrary to your thinking, which allows you to see the whole picture from God's perspective. A properly planted dream enables the dreamer to dialogue with God.

EXERCISES

A. What is the difference between planting a dream in the soul realm versus the spiritual realm?

Discussion

B. Do you trust God completely that He sees your circumstances from His perfect perspective?

Discussion

C. How and when will you begin to plant your dreams in the spirit?

Discussion

Actively Dreaming

POINTS TO NOTE

1. Dreaming can become active as you cooperate and allow God to further His communication with you. **No one can initiate a dream discussion with God**, but once He begins a conversation in dreams, I believe that you can take it further with Him. All believers should aim to further their dream communication ability with God, as He rewards every effort we make to get closer to Him (see Heb. 5:12-14; 11:6).

   God did this so that they would seek him and perhaps reach out for him and find him, though he is not far from any one of us. "For in him we live and move and have our being." As some of your own poets have said, "We are his offspring" (Acts 17:27-28).

2. If you pay attention to your dreams, respond appropriately, and diligently seek God's face, then your dreams will increase with greater detail, more explained mysteries, more impartation of divine power, and greater understanding of your nightly encounters.

EXERCISES

A. Do you regard dreaming as a passive or active aspect of your spiritual life?

Discussion

B. Although only God can initiate a dream discussion, do you believe you can take it further with Him, to get closer to Him? How?

Discussion

C. Write Acts 17:27-28 in your own words.

Discussion

A Living Encounter with Him

POINTS TO NOTE

1. One of God's primary objectives in communicating in dreams and visions is to establish a heart-to-heart connection with you. It is God's desire for you to experience the realities of who He is, even on your worst day. God wants you to have a living encounter with Him so you can imbibe His true attributes.

2. Dreams are valuable because their visual impact lingers in your spirit and flows into your memory. God may also dramatize His Word in dreams, making certain portions of Scripture come alive to you as real and living. The first step in advancing your dream life is to ask for more dreams.

3. Visualizing imagery in the Bible trains your mind to understand the Word of God, which comes with enough spiritual power to transform your mind for better understanding of His ways. Dreams increase your knowledge of God and His heart. As you spend more time studying the Word of God, your dream life will become more clear and rich.

EXERCISES

A. Do you have a heart-to-heart connection with God, even on your worst day?

Discussion

B. Has God ever dramatized His Word in dreams, making Scripture passages come alive to you as real and living?

Discussion

C. As you spend more time studying the Word of God, your dream life will become more clear and rich. Are you ready for that reality?

Discussion

PRACTICAL PRINCIPLES AND DISCUSSION

CHAPTER 6

Wisdom from God

POINTS TO NOTE

1. Phrases in Dreams and Visions from God are often clear, short, and sharp. They may require prompt attention and action. They usually come with little ambiguity. Dream phrases should be recorded exactly as you have heard them because their divine insights may run beyond the limits of human reasoning. Dream phrases that run contrary to Scripture are not from God, no matter how smooth, appropriate, alluring, or wise they may sound. Commonly, decreed events come with or through dream phrases in the Bible.

2. Voices in your dreams should be carefully discerned. The voice of God will bear witness with the dreamer's spirit, like a knowing in the inner being that God is stirring something within (see John 10:4-5; 1 John 2:20). You have the Holy Spirit anointing and the seal of God within to tell you the truth. Even statements from angels need to be judged as Galatians 1:8 warns.

   But even if we or an angel from heaven should preach a gospel other than the one we preached to you, let them be under God's curse!

3. Sometimes phrases from the second heaven—the domain of the devil and his agents—will occur in the dream experiences. What was said will not sit well with you, or you will have a deep reservation about the information. Subject every dream phrase to the following tests: *Does it line up with Scripture? Does it pass the love test? Does it pass the wisdom test? The ultimate test for wisdom from God is the revelation that we should have respect for human lives, no matter whose life is involved.*

EXERCISES

A. You have the Holy Spirit anointing and the seal of God within to tell you the truth. Open your heart and spirit to hear His truth.

   ### Discussion

B. Every dream phrase needs to be subjected to the three tests—this is important to remember.

Discussion

C. Why do you think that the ultimate test for wisdom from God is if the revelation has respect for human lives?

Discussion

Expanding the Scope of Your Dreams

POINTS TO NOTE

1. The "scope of your dreams" is the total area of coverage in your dreams; dreams about personal issues and dreams that have no direct personal relevance. Most dreamers dream mainly of personal issues. The scope of your dreams also includes sensitivity of the information and security of its content. Determine the percentage of your dreams that relate to you, relate to others, and relate to you and others. Some estimates state that about 95 percent of a person's dreams relate to his or her own life.
2. People with a "watchman anointing" (more about this topic in Part III of this training manual) have a widened scope that includes their area of calling; *then a good percentage of their dreams would relate to other people.*
3. The watchman may need help in managing personal issues, while also dreaming of strategic insights into the enemy's plans and the path lying ahead for the Church. Dreamers who pay attention to others and then intercede for them will naturally have their dream scope widened. What you spend time on, you make room for!
4. When God begins speaking to you in dreams regarding others, it's usually a result of your increasing concern for their welfare. Perhaps this explains why your immediate family members frequently turn up in your dreams!

EXERCISES

A. Define the scope of your dreams in your own words.

Discussion

B. Do you want to expand the scope of your dreams? Why or why not?

Discussion

C. Do you most frequently dream about family members, your life, or others?

Discussion

Managing Sensitive and Secure Information

POINTS TO NOTE

1. The sensitivity and security content of a dream reflects the trust God has in you. God will trust you with sensitive information concerning your life in the following order:

   Potential events: what is likely to happen, but is not inevitable in your life.

   Decreed events: what God has ordained to happen, no matter what, in your life.

   God's sovereign plan for the dreamer: the very reason for your life experiences.

2. Many dreamers misuse such privileged revelation and become arrogant about the good promises given by God—doing so compromises and delays fulfillment of a promise. Public pronouncement of a personal promise must be solely for building up the other people.

3. You must realize that not all revelations are ready for public pronouncement. Timing is a key factor. God Himself told Daniel, *"But you, Daniel, close up and seal the words of the scroll until the time of the end. Many will go here and there to increase knowledge"* (Dan. 12:4; see also Neh. 2:12-13).

4. If God can trust you with sensitive information about your life or ministry, then He will progress to trust you with information about other people. He will first begin with potential events; follow with decreed events, and then conclude with His sovereign plans for them. If these levels are well-managed, then God will entrust you with knowledge about other people's weaknesses for the purpose of intercession. This sequence is common but it is by no means cast in iron.

EXERCISES

A. Have you received sensitive information in the following order: *potential events; decreed events; God's sovereign plan for the dreamer?*

Discussion

B. Have you misused privileged revelation or become arrogant about the good promises given by God?

Discussion

C. Can God trust you with sensitive information concerning your life or ministry?

Discussion

Crossing Over to the Dark Side?

POINTS TO NOTE

1. Sin, disobedience, and wrong motivation have a profound impact on your gifts. For example, disobedience leads to rebellion; in such a place of darkness, a gifted person can draw power from the satanic network. If giftedness is corrupted, a gifted person can cross over from operating in divine power to the power of darkness. The dividing line can often be quite fine.
2. Many biblical examples exist of this crossover phenomenon. A classic example is the life of King Saul. Since the gifts of God are irrevocable, it is not uncommon for gifted people to stray into the domain of evil power and still show evidence of giftedness. Saul was once anointed of God (see 1 Sam. 10:9-11).
3. Due to disobedience and rebellion, Saul allowed himself to be dragged into a life of bitterness, jealousy, unforgiveness, and vengeance. An evil spirit affected his physical life and permeated his spiritual walk with God (see 1 Sam. 28:5-8).
4. Many gifted people have unknowingly become corrupted. Rather than receiving revelation from God, they operate in satanic evil. Many New Agers actually have God's gifts, but they have crossed over to power from the dark side.

EXERCISES

A. Have you witnessed a believer whose disobedience led to rebellion and crossing over to the dark side?

Discussion

B. Lust for money and things of the world have caused many to cross over into divination. Name a few modern-day crossovers—pray for them.

Discussion

C. Are you familiar with New Age philosophy or do you know people who are New Agers? How do their beliefs differ from yours?

Discussion

True Dreams, Visions, and Prophecies Correlate

POINTS TO NOTE

1. True dreams, visions, and prophecies on the same subject do not contradict one another because they originate from one single Source. Dreams and visions in the Bible follow this pattern, regardless of the time, place, or people group involved. All true prophecies correlate and are inspired by the Holy Spirit (see 1 Cor. 14:33 AMP; Rev. 19:10b TLB; 2 Cor. 13:1; 2 Pet. 1:19).
2. Sometimes people connected in some way receive the same message, although dramatized with individual characteristics. For instance, a river bursting its banks may be in dreams of several people living within a specific geographical location. This could reflect a divine message in the people's spiritual atmosphere. Scriptural examples include Genesis 40:2-23 and Daniel 2 and 7.

EXERCISES

A. What other aspects of the spiritual reality can you trace back to the Holy Spirit?

Discussion

B. What type of feelings does reading Second Peter 1:19 bring to your spirit surface?

Discussion

C. A river bursting its banks may be in dreams of people living within a specific geographical location. Do you have personal examples like this?

Discussion

The Gift of Interpreting Dreams—Spirit of Wisdom Offshoot

POINTS TO NOTE

1. The gift of interpreting dreams is an offshoot of the spirit of wisdom, which is a special type of divine wisdom given to understand God's mind in sending a true dream by the Holy Spirit. The gift of interpretation is often associated with the spirit of counsel and administrative ability. The "power of proclamation" can also be given to a gifted interpreter (see 1 Cor. 12:7-8; Gen. 40:8).
2. The connection between the gift of interpretation and the spirit of wisdom is evident in Daniel 1:20, Daniel 5:11-12 and Daniel 5:15-16.
3. When speaking of Joseph's wisdom and his associated ability to interpret dreams, *"Pharaoh said to Joseph, 'Since God has made all this known to you, there is no one so discerning and wise as you. You shall be in charge of my palace, and all my people are to submit to your orders. Only with respect to the throne will I be greater than you'"* (Gen. 41:39-40).

EXERCISES

A. Why do you think that the gift of interpretation is often associated with the spirit of counsel and administrative ability?

Discussion

B. In all the Scripture passages cited, in which one is the connection between the gift of interpretation and the spirit of wisdom most evident?

Discussion

C. From where did Joseph's wisdom come?

Discussion

PRACTICAL PRINCIPLES AND DISCUSSION

CHAPTER 7

The Gift of Interpretation

Gaining Proficiency in Interpreting Dreams

POINTS TO NOTE

1. Only people who remember dreams on a consistent basis become proficient at skillfully interpreting dreams. Therefore, the gift of interpretation can be regarded as an offshoot of a prophetic anointing. Individuals who receive dreams and remember them consistently can be said to have a "prophetic slant to their gift."
2. A dream's covert meaning actually exists in the dreamer's spirit, but it may be unfruitful to the dreamer's mind until a true interpretation is given. With correct interpretation, the dreamer will usually acknowledge trustworthiness of that interpretation.
3. An interpreter needs to get familiar with the dreamer's circumstance, *as most dreams are divine responses to the questions in the heart of the dreamer.* The interpreter should know the preoccupation of the dreamer. God uses what the dreamer is familiar with to explain what the dreamer may not yet know. *Interpret symbols from the world the dreamer is familiar with*; symbols may derive meaning from the dreamer's life experience.

EXERCISES

A. The gift of interpretation can be enhanced and intensified by: studying the Word of God; keeping a pure conscience; laying aside personal agendas; surrendering your will; and living in constant communion with God. Are you committed to this regimen?

Discussion

B. If you receive dreams and remember them consistently, do you consider yourself "prophetic"?

Discussion

C. Should you seek interpretation of a covert meaning of a dream?

Discussion

Word of Knowledge Interpretation

POINTS TO NOTE

1. All true interpretation comes with the Holy Spirit's help; its actual outworking is either through a word of knowledge, a gift of interpretation, or a process of acquired interpretative skills. A word of knowledge is the spiritual gift of knowing 'information' beyond natural means, as through God's revelation: *"To one there is given through the Spirit a message of wisdom, to another a message of knowledge by means of the same Spirit"* (1 Cor. 12:8). Word of knowledge is always about the past and the present, while the prophecy speaks of the future.

2. Many prophetic people interpret dreams by a word of knowledge rather than acquired interpretative skills. Such people often cannot explain how they arrived at an interpretation on the basis of a dream's elements. When God gives interpretation by word of knowledge, He sows its meaning into a person's mind without necessarily expounding on the relevance of the dream's elements (symbolism).

3. Some people awake from dreams with a prompting to a specific Bible passage. This is the result of God's sowing the relevant Scripture into the dreamer's mind. Word of knowledge interpretation, however, usually does not explain the relevance of a dream's elements to the life circumstances of the dreamer; it is restricted in details. However, there is enough detail to keep the dreamer from falling into a disastrous mistake, but every word of knowledge interpretation should be complemented with an acquired skill of interpretation.

4. Word of knowledge interpretation gives only a certain percentage of a dream's full meaning; therefore, it's short on intended keys of wisdom inherent in dreams. However, such interpretation is nearly always the correct essence of its message. Most angelic interpretations in the Bible appear to be word of knowledge

interpretations; yet, if asked, the angels usually also gave further exposition on elements of the dreams or visions. Having a word of knowledge is the most common way that dreamers with undeveloped interpretative skills can gain understanding of dreams.

EXERCISES

A. Do you have the spiritual gift of a word of knowledge?

Discussion

B. Have you been awakened from a dream with a prompting to a specific Bible passage?

Discussion

C. Cite a few times when angelic interpretations in the Bible appear to be word of knowledge interpretations and the angels gave further exposition on elements of the dreams or visions.

Discussion

Three Ways to Interpret Your Dreams

POINTS TO NOTE

1. God helps you interpret your dreams in these three ways:

   - Giving word of knowledge regarding His mind in sending the dream.
   - The gift of interpretation.
   - Acquiring interpretative skills.

2. There are also various combinations of these three:

   - Word of knowledge plus acquired skills is the most common combination. Most people in some form of prophetic ministry will use this mode.
   - Gift of interpretation and acquired skills comprise people with a gift of interpretation who have made the effort to develop that gifting. These are people with a Daniel-type anointing. Remember, Daniel was not only gifted, but was also skilled at learning and gaining knowledge (see Dan. 1:17).
   - Gift of interpretation without acquiring skills of interpretation applies to people who make no effort to acquire more skills at interpreting dreams even though gifted by God.

3. All revelation needs some form of interpretation, whether symbolic or literal, or perhaps a combination of the two. All of these forms of interpretation may be applied to a single revelation. Allow only logical deduction from what has been revealed. Do not get bogged down with rigid application of types and symbols; instead, practice a broad principle of interpretation. Although you have received a revelation, you may not automatically receive interpretation, which always comes as determined by the Holy Spirit.

4. One crucial point: interpretation should come into your mind by a gradual inflow of the Holy Spirit; true interpretation does not come by intensive or rigorous reasoning. After receiving prompting from the Holy Spirit, the interpreter should apply minimal reasoning to elaborate.

EXERCISES

A. Is it hard for you to avoid assumption and only allow logical deduction from what has been revealed about your dream?

Discussion

B. Even though you have received a revelation, you may not automatically receive its interpretation, which always come from the Holy Spirit who determines when to give the meaning.

Discussion

C. True interpretation does not come by intense or rigorous reasoning; apply only minimal reasoning to elaborate.

Discussion

True and Complete Interpretation

POINTS TO NOTE

1. Only God has the complete picture. Any true interpretation will allow for expansion of understanding and will be consistent with future progressive revelation on the subject.

2. *Exposition brings understanding to symbols and events as they relate to the dreamer's personal experience*. Deriving meaning for symbols must go along with the exposition to truly interpret a dream or vision. True and complete interpretation of a symbol must take the following into consideration:

    - Scripture
    - The inherent meaning of the symbol
    - The dreamer's personal experience
    - The social influences of the dreamer (such as the culture and colloquial expressions that he or she is used to)

3. You should not advocate a formula-based approach to dream interpretation. Reliance on the Holy Spirit is an absolute necessity. However, I have found the following to be helpful:

    - Wait for the prompting of the Holy Spirit. Correct interpretation does not come by human reasoning, but an inflow into our hearts or subconscious from God.
    - Understand the meaning of the symbols and actions.
    - Explain the relevance of events and symbols to the dreamer's circumstance.

4. Always put together a possible storyline for the dream. The plot should assemble the dream's elements and events without contradiction. The follows is helpful in determining whether the storyline is correct:

    - All elements will agree with or fit into the plot.
    - All actions will fit into the context of the plot.
    - Even if only one or two elements do not fit with the plot while the majority of others are in agreement, then the derived "meaning" of the symbol is not the appropriate one. Check other meanings of the symbol.
    - Declare God's sovereign message in the dream with the Holy Spirit's help. The proclamation must be based on why the interpreter perceives that God sent the message. It includes the interpreter's attempt to declare God's mind in sending a vision. Unfortunately, most dreamers are satisfied with just seeing dreams come to pass. But some dreams and visions may be given for the purpose of influencing future events; intercession can avert judgment or bring promises into reality.
    - Application *is bringing the message and the dream's wisdom to practical usefulness in the dreamer's life.*

EXERCISES

A. If deriving meaning for symbols should be predominantly centered on the Word of God, how familiar are you with His Word?

Discussion

B. Why shouldn't you rely on a formula-based approach to dream interpretation? Discussion

C. Does putting together a possible storyline for your dream sound fun or intimidating?

Discussion

Symbols

POINTS TO NOTE

1. To interpret a dream, you must think symbolically. A symbol's meaning must be revealed to the dreamer for each dream, as the same symbol may be different for distinct dreams. One meaning of a symbol is not necessarily its meaning for all dreams. Do not get fixed on a symbol's single meaning because it may change as you grow in your walk with God. As you study the Word of God, you will draw less on your own life experience and more from a biblical reservoir of examples.
2. Familiar symbols from your life experiences may have unique associations. Symbols are specific and purposeful. Particular symbols do not represent God's communication with you; such as being enticed by a prostitute is not the move of God, rather a temptation of your flesh.

3. The biblical understanding of symbols takes precedence over any other possible meaning. The meaning of symbolic actions is drawn primarily from your background, but should never contradict spiritual principles. Symbols in dreams are chosen for very specific purposes, so you must first identify God's purpose for using a particular symbol.

4. A dream's elements are symbolic in most cases, but some can be literal. There is a higher percentage of symbolic dreams than literal dreams. Actions in dreams are typically symbolic as well. The *context* of the dream is the circumstance in which events occur, or its sequence of events. *The background* is the setting or place in which the dream occurs.

EXERCISES

A. *Temptation* by the desire of your flesh is not from God, what are other symbols that would not represent a move of God?

Discussion

B. Dream symbols are chosen for very specific purposes; you must first identify God's purpose for using a particular symbol.

Discussion

C. What is the difference between the *context* and the *background* of dreams?

Discussion

Three Levels of Dream Interpretation Skills

POINTS TO NOTE

1. Human attempts to interpret dreams fall into one of three category levels: 0, 1, or 2.

- **Level 0** is the attempt by non-believers to interpret dreams.
- **Level 1** is a believer's compilation of dictionary-derived meaning of symbols, without any prompting of the Holy Spirit.
- **Level 2** is the true interpretation, as prompted by the Holy Spirit.

2. Here are two key Bible texts relevant for this categorization: First Corinthians 2:10-12 and Mark 4:11-12. True interpretation is being able to reveal the reason in God's mind in sending the dream. A true and complete interpretation will always answer the question: "Why did God send the dream?"
3. In the later part of life, Joseph operated at the Level 2 category. But in his younger days, he remained ignorant of the spiritual principle that public pronouncement of diving revelations should only be to bring about change in a positive way; it should never be done for self-aggrandizement. Joseph took thirteen years to reach Level 2. *(For more detailed discussion on this topic, see Dreams and Visions Volume 1, Chapter 13.)*

EXERCISES

A. What level do you fit into right now? What level do you aspire to reach?

Discussion

____

____

____

B. How do you interpret the passages from First Corinthians and Mark? Do they apply personally to you?

Discussion

____

____

____

C. What is the difference between how Joseph handled his dream interpretation when he was a youngster compared with his revelations while in prison and with the Pharaoh?

Discussion

PRACTICAL PRINCIPLES AND DISCUSSION

CHAPTER 8

Improving Your Interpretative Skills

POINTS TO NOTE

1. The following steps are not a complete dream interpretation formula. Always remember:

- Interpretation comes from God.
- Commit everything to God in prayer.
- You can receive interpretation instantaneously and/or through fasting/prayers/meditation, which brings clarity.
- Experience and the degree of your giftedness can influence how quickly interpretation is received.

Step 1

Listen in the spirit:

- Calm your soul in the Lord's presence.
- Use the eyes of your faith.
- Trust that God will give you the understanding.
- Allow the peace of God to rule your mind and heart.
- Wait for the prompting of the Holy Spirit.

Put away acts of the soulish realm:

- Do not allow intellectualism and logic to rule your mind.
- Do not entertain fear and confusion.
- Do not be apprehensive or anxious.
- Do not allow emotions from the dream to cloud your judgment.
- Keep a clear mind.

Step 2

Allow the essence of its message to flow into your spirit from God.

The Holy Spirit lights up an aspect of the dream that grabs your attention or imagination—this could be a symbol or an action in the dream—and the rest of the storyline will hinge upon this. Therefore, be sensitive and see what stands out in the dream or vision.

Look up the following examples of how the Holy Spirit will usually prompt you: Daniel 2:36-38; Daniel 7:19-21; Daniel 7:8; Daniel 7:11. God prompted Daniel by highlighting the boastful horn.

The following is helpful in characterizing a prompting from the Holy Spirit:

- Every element in the dream will agree with this prompting.
- Its context, trends, and background will line up with the prompting.
- The prompting should be capable of guiding an eventual, logical exposition of the dream's symbol and events.
- The plot or essence of the dream's message hinges on this prompting.

Step 3

Allow minimal logical process.

After receiving God's prompting, minimally use logical deductions to form the entire story correctly. Interpretation of a personal dream is often hindered by using logic first instead of receiving God's *rhema* word. The intrusion of preconceived ideas lead to clouded judgment. An example of permissible logical deduction after receiving prompting from the Holy Spirit is found in Daniel 2:39-42.

Step 4

Determine who/what the dream is about.

- A person
- A group of persons
- A place

Determine what aspect of the person's life is referred to in the dream.

The aspect of a dreamer's life that is addressed in a dream is usually reflected as its background setting:

- An office background usually represents a secular career.
- A family setting primarily indicates the personal life, bloodline, or generation.
- Church background relates to dreamer's ministry.
- Money speaks of favor from God, or actual money.

Determine the timing.

Unless specified, timing is usually fairly difficult to determine in dreams. Generally, the following will determine if a dream relates to past, present, or future:

- Old house: objects in the past influencing the present.
- Clocks: lateness or presumption, depending on whether it indicates being late or early.
- Dates: as relevant to the actual date.
- Time of day, in terms of morning, afternoon, and evening.

Step 5

The interpreter intimates with the dreamer.

The interpreter should also ask the same questions that the sailors asked Jonah: *"...What do you do? Where do you come from? What is your country? From what people are you?"* (Jon. 1:8). Also confirm if there are any preoccupations in the dreamer's mind.

Step 6

Determine the plot of the dream.

Determining the plot leads to the unraveling of the dream's superior wisdom.

Step 7

The dreamer should confirm the interpretation.

God may speak confirmation in many ways: an audible voice; a still small voice; dreams and visions; mental pictures; and inner impressions. Confirmation can also happen in other forms of prophecies, through prophets, events (past or ongoing), and other revelatory means from God, including recurring dreams.

Step 8

The dreamer should take responsibility for what is revealed.

Take action on the confirmed interpretation, even if it is only to meditate and pray on what has been revealed.

Step 9

Above all, let the glory go to God.

God used Joseph and Daniel to reveal the meaning of dreams. Both were quick to acknowledge God alone as the One who gave them the ability to interpret dreams. God alone deserves all the glory (see Gen. 41:15-16 and Daniel 2:27,30).

EXERCISES

A. How does the Holy Spirit usually prompt you?

Discussion

B. Out of the nine steps listed, which one is the easiest for you to follow? Which is the hardest?

Discussion

C. Do you, or will you, always give God the glory for the interpretation?

Discussion

PRACTICAL PRINCIPLES AND DISCUSSION

CHAPTER 9

The Language of the Spirit

POINTS TO NOTE

1. The language of the spirit is symbolic; no other book speaks in symbols more than the Bible. The language pattern of dreams is similar to the pattern of speech used in the Bible. Because of its extensive symbolism, some have described the Old Testament as the New Testament concealed.
2. The language of *reason* is limited, whereas the language of *symbols* is infinite. A symbol may be identified by one word, yet may take volumes to be comprehensively described. The language of symbols and symbolic actions has great depth and power. Humankind thinks and processes information in pictures because the language of symbols is richer than words (see Num. 12:6-8).
3. Jesus Christ explained why He spoke in parables to the people in Matthew 13:10-13 and Mark 4:33-34. He revealed secrets of God's Kingdom only to the disciples. The Holy Spirit helps explains God's symbolic language of dark speeches, similitude, and parables. Without the Holy Spirit's help, you will not understand the mind of God on any issue.

EXERCISES

A. How attune are you to the symbolic language of the Spirit?

Discussion

B. Does it frustrate you that God chooses to speak in parables and uses symbols?

Discussion

C. Dependence on the Holy Spirit for explanation is the key to understanding.

Discussion

Why God Uses Symbols

POINTS TO NOTE

1. There are several reasons why God uses symbols:

   - To help you see the real situation from God's perspective.
   - Symbols help impartation and interpretation.
   - The hidden meaning of a symbol allows God to clarify in stages.
   - Humility when seeking meaning increases your dependence on the Holy Spirit.
   - Symbols bring specificity because dreams are an intimate form of communication between you and the Lord.
   - Symbolism secures the message from the enemy.
   - It makes you want to discover the meaning.
   - The language of symbols is deep and powerful and our most elementary language, available to all ages.
   - The human mind understands and reads in pictures.

2. Those who understand the tremendous power of symbolism gain incredible insights into God's mysteries; His ways are wrapped up in symbolic language. Because people tend to think in pictures, symbols evoke powerful emotion and elicit strong passion.

EXERCISES

A. Is there a certain Christian symbol that holds great meaning for you?

Discussion

B. What secular symbols come to mind that have very worldly connotations?

Discussion

C. What symbol dishonored would outrage you?

Discussion

Symbolism Overtones

POINTS TO NOTE

1. Symbolism was used to reveal David's adulterous act to him. God chose Nathan to narrate the message to David in dream format—of a parable—to reveal the gravity of David's sin (see 2 Sam. 12:1-9). Nathan reveals to King David that he is the man who has committed the crime, and that God is judging him for the murder of Uriah the Hittite and his adultery with Bathsheba.
2. A dream is God's picture language interlaced with words. No one can understand dreams correctly without some understanding of the Bible's symbols, metaphors, and speech patterns. Until you understand symbolic connotations, many elements in dreams will remain unexpressed.

3. When you come across an image and truly switch to symbolic thinking, two questions should arise in your mind:

    - What is the literal meaning of the image? (Usually the most obvious meaning.)
    - What does the image evoke? (These are the overtones.) If either of these aspects is not well understood, your comprehension of the pictorial language is limited.

An Example:

Husband:

1. Ordinarily understood to mean male or man.
2. The word also evokes some lateral thinking of father, head of a home, provider, or God.

EXERCISES

A. Have you been corrected or judged by God as was David?

Discussion

B. How easy is it for you to switch to symbolic thinking?

Discussion

C. After considering the husband example, can you think of other examples? Write several.

Discussion

Benefits of Parable Language

The benefits of understanding parable language include:

- Economy—a picture is worth a thousand words.
- The essence is revealed as you apply specifics to your situation. Also gives the principle so the essence can be applicable at other times.
- A parable allows God to code messages for the dreamer.
- The promise is protected because the dream hides it from the enemy.
- Allows God to package and unfold His message according to areas of priority (see Hosea 12:10).
- The language of pictures and symbols is universal and has no age barrier.
- Allows God to give the best possible picture or truest perspective of a situation.
- A dream parable often shows the present condition, and predicts what will happen if you continue in the same direction.

The purpose of the parable language is explained in Proverbs 1:1-6 (AMP).

EXERCISES

A. Can you think of additional benefits of the parable language?

Discussion

B. What truth stands out most to you in the Proverbs 1:1-6 passage?

Discussion

C. What pictures come to your mind when you hear the phrases the crucifixion of Christ and Christ's resurrection?

Discussion

Outworkings of the Spirit

1. The following are ways in which the Holy Spirit manifests His presence within His body:

- ***Burning*** or persistent nudge (see Luke 9:45; 24:13-16, 30-32).
- ***Still small voice*** (see 1 Kings 19:11-13).
- ***Voice behind you*** (see Isa. 30:21).
- ***Gentle resistance or push.*** Apostle Paul said the Holy Spirit forbade him; the Bible also says God resists the proud (see James 4:6; 1 Peter 5:5).
- ***Carried by the Spirit.*** Ezekiel was carried by the Spirit (see Ezek. 37 and 2 Peter 1:21: *"For no prophecy ever originated because some man willed it [to do so—it never came by human impulse], but men spoke from God who were borne along (moved and impelled) by the Holy Spirit"* (AMP).
- ***In the Spirit*** (see Rev. 1:10; 4:1-2, prayers, worshiping; Acts 13:1-3, music; 2 Kings 3:14-17, company, atmosphere, fasting, spontaneous).
- ***Quickening*** (see Prov. 24:30-32).
- ***Birthing or flight of ideas*** (see Luke 21:15). Word of wisdom, an offshoot of spiritual wisdom; for example, Solomon's idea of dividing the living child between the two quarreling women.
- ***Overwhelming or almost complete take-over*** (Mary, see Luke 1:35; Disciples, see Acts 2:1-2).
- ***Physical manifestations:*** Groaning that no one can understand; laughing; crying; dancing; weirdness (see 2 Cor. 12:3, "...whether in the body or out of the body I do not know...").

EXERCISES

A. How many ways have you personally seen or felt the Holy Spirit manifested? What was your reaction?

Discussion

B. Of the ways listed, which three would you prefer the Holy Spirit use to make His presence known to you?

Discussion

C. Have you had any physical manifestations such as the ones mentioned? Are they rare occurrences or frequent? Public or private?

Discussion

PRACTICAL PRINCIPLES AND DISCUSSION

CHAPTER 10

Common Dream Situations

The following common dream situations are worthy of more detail and specific aspects at this point in the manual. The more you know about your dreams the better you can use them to benefit yourself, others, and glorify God. This chapter gives you the tools to not only make sense of revelations, but also provides steps to take in responding and applying the wisdom gained from your dreams.

Repeated Dreams

- Dreams repeated more than once within a short time—commonly occur in a single night.
- May be minor variations in elements or symbolic actions within the dreams, but plot remains the same.
- See Pharaoh's dreams in Genesis 41:1-8.
- Dreams are repeated for the following reasons:

1. For divine insights into other aspects that might have been missed.
2. Decreed events that God has ordained to happen. Joseph said dreams can be repeated when the event is settled in Heaven. Such dreams will soon happen: *"The reason the dream was given to Pharaoh in two forms is that the matter has been firmly decided by God, and God will do it soon"* (Gen. 41:32).

Recurring Dreams

Recurring dreams are repeated more than twice over a long period of time and often indicate an issue that needs to be resolved or is in the process of resolution. For example, see Joseph's dream in Genesis 37:1-15. Dreams can recur because of:

- Hurts or unhealed wounds of the past.
- Emotional scars that need healing.
- Bondages or negative strongholds that need to be pulled down.
- Divine insights into other aspects of the matter that might have been missed.
- Persistent misunderstanding or partial understanding of a message from a previous dream.
- No responses or inappropriate responses to previous dreams.

- Once a recurring dream has been correctly interpreted and its meaning acted upon, then the dream will usually not recur.

Nightmares and Night Terror

Read: Job 7:13 AMP; Job 33:13-18 AMP.

- A nightmare is a dream that arouses feelings of acute fear, dread, or anguish. It is a subjective term reflecting the dreamer's perception and judgment. This is why children are more prone to call dreams "nightmares." Some may regard the following as nightmares:
- Dreams that have become more graphic because the dreamer has not listened to previous subtle dream warnings. If the dreamer fails to respond, a frightening nightmare shows how serious the situation has become.
- Dreams of spiritual warfare often warn the dreamer about hell's assignments and reveal a divine strategy for victory.
- Dreams that warn of impending dangers may address personal weaknesses or the likelihood of poor judgment that may lead to bad decisions or warn of the danger of wrong associations or influences.
- King Nebuchadnezzar had a terrifying dream that told him about his kingdom's future (see Dan. 2:1-3).
- Job was warned in dreams though he did not understand them, *"For God does speak—now one way, now another—though man may not perceive it"* (Job 33:13). The dreams gradually became a nightmare to Job: *"When I think my bed will comfort me and my couch will ease my complaint, even then you frighten me with dreams and terrify me with visions..."* (Job 7:13-14).

Handling Nightmares/Night Terrors

The correct handling depends on the type of spiritual encounter and what is possibly the cause of the revelation terror.

Consider in what spiritual experience it occurred.

- In twilight experience, then it is often a wake up call, an urgent need to act, or it is referring to a happening event.
- In visionary experience, more commonly real and literal plans and actions of the devil or contrary to the will of God.
- In dream experience, often symbolic reference either to a warning, personal weakness or unhealed hurt or negative stronghold.

Consider what may be the possible source of the terror:

- Revelations about spiritual warfare *(often come in dreams, a call to prayers)*
- Revelations of the plans of hell against you *(often come in visions or twilight states, an urgent call prayers)*

- Revelations about your weaknesses *(often come in dreams, a call to self-check, repentance and prayers)*
- Other warning such impending wrong decision *(often come in dreams, a call to truthfulness and prayers)*
- Negative stronghold that needs to be addressed *(often come in dreams, call for intercession)*

Deliverance and Nightmares

Deliverance from recurring nightmares is possible under the following premise:

- To break the fear or phobia or insecurity that may come as backlash from the nightmare.
- To break any negative stronghold, past experiences, or root of bitterness that may be the cause of the nightmares or that is being addressed (revealed) in the nightmares.
- To cast out any demon that might have gained entrance by any of the above.
- To re-educate to bring proper godly perspectives to the situation. Otherwise attempts at deliverance from the nightmare could be protracted and ineffective.

Responding to Your Dreams

Steps to Take

- Allow peace to reign in your mind immediately upon awaking.
- Avoid emotional backlash.
- Ask God to help you remember what you saw during the night.
- Allow the dream to flow into your mind.
- Try to rerun events as they played out in the dream. This helps to transcribe the message into more permanent memory ink.
- Write down the dream and study it.
- Pray about all elements, events, and circumstances of the dream.
- Do not act on the dream before its interpretation is confirmed.
- When the dream's meaning has been confirmed, first begin by making only minor adjustments toward the dream's fulfillment.
- Start with what will not drastically alter your personal circumstance.
- Remember, obedience is better than sacrifice.
- As you obey with the small, God will unfold greater responsibility.
- Allow your faith to gradually build up before you take the stake to a higher level.

- Always remember that dreams are possibilities—not inevitabilities.
- A dream may not always sound logical, but hang on to it and treasure it until the appointed time: *"But Mary treasured up all these things and pondered them in her heart"* (Luke 2:19). *"When he told his father as well as his brothers, his father rebuked him and said, 'What is this dream you had? Will your mother and I and your brothers actually come and bow down to the ground before you?' His brothers were jealous of him, but his father kept the matter in mind"* (Genesis 37:10-11).
- Dreams always lead to a process. Identify the direction to which you are drawn. An appropriate interpretation should bring you closer to God—to Him, the journey is as important as the destination. God measures maturity and character, but the dreamer may be more conscious of progress as a measure of time.
- Respond truthfully to corrective dreams; it is between you and God.
- *"When I kept silent, my bones wasted away through my groaning all day long. For day and night Your hand was heavy on me; my strength was sapped as in the heat of summer. Then I acknowledged my sin to You and did not cover up my iniquity. I said, 'I will confess my transgressions to the Lord'—and You forgave the guilt of my sin"* (Psalm 32:3-5).

Responding to Warning Dreams

- A dreamer may receive dreams warning against an impending danger, errors in judgment, misplaced priorities, and life-changing situations.
- Warning dreams are usually so prayers can be offered and calamity averted. *"Is that the right reply for you to make, O House of Jacob? Do you think the spirit of the Lord likes to talk to you so roughly? No! His threats are for your good, to get on the path again"* (Micah 2:7 TLB).
- Remain calm and do not jump to hasty conclusions.
- Quiet your soul before the Lord,
- Ask the Lord to bring His peace and further divine revelation on the subject.
- The purpose of the warning is to make intercession and avert judgment. Nebuchadnezzar did not heed the advice that Daniel had given him, so calamity eventually overtook him. *"'Therefore, O king, be pleased to accept my advice: Renounce your sins by doing what is right, and your wickedness by being kind to the oppressed. It may be that then your prosperity will continue.' All this happened to King Nebuchadnezzar. Twelve months later, as the king was walking on the roof of the royal palace of Babylon, he said, 'Is not this the great Babylon I have built as the royal residence, by my mighty power and for the glory of my majesty?' The words were still on his lips when a voice came from heaven, 'This is what is decreed for you, King Nebuchadnezzar: Your royal authority has been taken from you...'"* (Daniel 4:27-31).
- Many become terrified instead of being thankful for advance notice and a chance to avert danger.
- Seek healing for any areas of fear that the dream might have stirred up.

- Ask God to eliminate any stronghold of fear from your life and to remove any emotional backlash from your soul.
- Always remember that it's only a warning!

Life Application and Appropriation of Dreams

- Only confirmed, correctly interpreted dreams should be applied.
- First, simply apply the dream and its symbols to yourself even when the dream speaks of other people.
- Start with simple changes that do not entail major shifts in your circumstances, unless the dream specifically says to do so.
- Always move according to the proportion of your faith—without faith, it is impossible to please God.
- Appropriate the dream.
- Appropriation is the process by which the dreamer in faith assumes or adopts the promise of the dream. Appropriation consists of: faith; diligent seeking, such as studying relevant Bible passages; preparing the soil of your heart by encouraging yourself in the Lord; paying attention to fine details.

Signs that the Interpretation Is Wrong

- It does not sit right with the dreamer—no inner witness.
- Causes strife, always emphasizes the negative, and takes away hope.
- Seeks self-interest—no respect for human life, especially the life of an enemy.
- Does not speak of love—drives the dreamer from God and seeks vengeance.
- Leads to bondage.
- Interpretative attempts are not based on biblical principles and cannot link a series of dreams on the same subject.
- The mind of God is not usually reflected.
- Misplaced priorities—does not have the wisdom of the Holy Spirit.
- Does not lead to a closer walk with God—may cause confusion.
- The dreamer's yearning is not satisfied.
- Creates fear and lack of faith.
- May be correct symbol meaning, but no relevance to the dreamer's life situation, and proclamation is wrong and ineffective.

Signs that the Interpretation Is Correct

- The dreamer acknowledges the true worthiness of the interpretation, as if God has spoken His wisdom into the situation.
- Speaks God's mind into the situation and gives clear, unambiguous instruction for the way forward.
- Bears relevance to the dreamer's circumstances.
- Always speaks of love.
- Leaves the dreamer with hope and builds up faith.
- It is truthful—even if it's a warning. Correctly links related series of dreams and brings appropriate exposition and proclamation.

Special Dream Situations

Babies in dreams – common with intercessors nurturing other young or challenged ministries

Toilets in dreams – common with intercessors; need to live a life of continuous repentance on behalf of everyone

Inability to speak or move in dreams – indicates the presence of evil spirit, attempts of the enemy to challenge the plans of God in the person's life

Sex in dreams – enticement or overindulgence in pleasures of life, may not be sexually related issues in some cases; repeated sex in dreams may be over preoccupation with sexual desire or unhealed sexual addiction

Lost in an otherwise familiar environment – may indicate indecision in the life of the dreamer; also common among older people

Repeated spiritual warfare dreams – may indicate watchman anointing

Summary

God used dreams and visions at critical points to guide and direct the lives of people and nations in those days. In the Old and New Testaments dreams carried special significance and are often a way God makes known His will to humankind. For instance, Joseph had dreams of his rulership many years before it was fulfilled; Abimelek, the Philistine king, was warned in a dream that Sarah was the wife of Abraham; Joseph, the earthly father of Jesus was encouraged to marry Mary, and later he was warned to take Mary and Jesus to Egypt when Jesus' life was in peril. Therefore, the Bible says, *"God, who at various times, and in various ways spoke in time past to the fathers by the prophets"* (Heb. 1:1 NKJV) in dreams (see Dan. 7:1-14), in visions (see Ezek. 8:4), by angels (see Zech. 19:9), by the burning bush (see Exod. 3:4), and by direct audible voice (see Gen. 12:1).

Concerning the present age, God says, *"If there is a prophet among you, I, the Lord, make Myself known to him in a vision; I speak to him in a dream"* (Num. 12:6).

And speaking of the future, God says, *"It shall come to pass in the last days, says God, that I will pour out of My Spirit on all flesh; your sons and daughters shall prophesy, your young men shall see visions and your old men shall dream dreams"* (Acts 2:17).

God spoke clearly in time past through dreams and visions, and at present He continues to speak through them and will speak through them in the future. We can no longer afford to be silent about our dreams. A great percentage of the members of every local church receives and ponders dreams and visions on a daily basis. Within every local Christian congregation is a thriving community of people desperate to find meaning for their nightly encounters. We must acknowledge their existence and do something to bring the light of God into the situation. The alternative is to sit back and allow innocent people to drift into darkness and into the hand of the prince of the darkness.

The world is continually flooded with rapidly expanding occult literature and misinformation about dreams and visions. Non-Christian literature is full of deception, profiteering, and confusion on this subject. We can no longer sit back and do nothing. The more the church distances itself from this valuable means of divine communication, the more erroneous and frustrating interpretation drives even honest Christians into spiritual bondage. Our greatest asset on earth is not only our ability to hear from God but also our ability to hear and understand what God says. Dreams and visions are ways God uses to direct our steps and bring His agenda of Heaven to the earth.

Modern lies and superstitious attitudes regarding dreams and visions are because all people experience them—Christians and non-Christians alike. Without the Holy Spirit, the majority of non-believers treats dreams and visions as omens and use them outside God's purposes. Such practices use godly principles in ungodly ways and are a form of fortunetelling. This has tainted the image of dreams and visions within the Christian community. We need to carefully restore this valuable means of divine communication using biblical methods.

PRACTICAL PRINCIPLES AND DISCUSSION

PART II

GET UNDERSTANDING

CHAPTER 11

Hearing Voices

POINTS TO NOTE

1. It is possible to gain clearer understanding of your dreams and visions and avail yourself of the valuable wisdom keys inherent in dreams and visions that you receive. The Bible says, *"In all your getting, get understanding"* (Prov. 4:7b). From the foundation of time, there has been a battle over gaining proper understanding and knowledge. God Himself lamented that, *"My people are destroyed for lack of knowledge"* (Hosea 4:6) and that His truth will set you free.
2. In the last days, believers will dream dreams and see visions, and there will also be a corresponding release of the spirit of understanding from the throne of God. God will pour out divining illumination for understanding these dreams and visions. Illuminating insights emanating from the doors of the third heaven will come upon the earth to bring explanation to the mysteries of God like never before.
3. The administration of this grace for divine understanding of the mysteries of God will come upon many servants of God in a new and fresh way. It is important to recognize when the Spirit of God brings simplicity to the things that have been regarded as complex over the ages.
4. It is time to leave shallow understanding of your dreams and visions and move into their proper and deeper understanding. You can maximize the benefits of the divine wisdom keys inherent in your dreams.

EXERCISES

A. The Spirit of God brings simplicity to perplexing issues. What complex issues do you need to take to the Lord for explanation?

Discussion

B. How can you maximize the benefits of the divine wisdom keys inherent in your dreams?

Discussion

C. What if the only thing the angel told Mary was that she was going to have a baby?

Discussion

Four Ways to Hear God's Voice

POINTS TO NOTE

1. The first voice Adam heard was the voice of God (see Gen. 2:16-17). There are four ways that people hear the voice of God:

- Some are *hearers*—their gift is predominantly in the ability to hear what God is saying.
- Some are *feelers*—they feel what God wants to communicate, such as feeling pain in the part of the body where God wants to heal someone.
- Some are *seers*—they are gifted in the ability to see pictures, flashes of pictures, and dreams and visions on a constant basis.
- Others are *spiritually sensitive* enough to discern what God is saying by the spirit of discernment.

2. No matter how you hear the voice of God, you must confirm that it is God. There are many voices in the spirit world, but the voice of God is easily recognizable if the message is subjected to the following checks. If it does, it's more than likely a message from God.

3. Does the message:

- Lead you to greater intimacy with God?
- Lead to expression of love? (God is love.)
- Put God's benefit and the interest of others before personal benefit?
- Lead to greater manifestations of Christ-likeness?
- Lead to more humility? Or does it appeal to the ego?
- Generate more joy, peace, and righteousness? (The Kingdom of God is love, peace and righteousness in the Holy Spirit.)
- Lead to greater dependence on God?
- Line up with the written Word of God?

EXERCISES

A. Are you a hearer, feeler, seer, or discerner? What makes you think so?

Discussion

B. Do you quickly and seriously ask yourself the questions mentioned to confirm whose voice you are hearing?

Discussion

C. Can you easily recognize God's voice?

Discussion

The Voice of Others

POINTS TO NOTE

1. The next voice Adam heard was that of Eve. The voice of Eve was the first human voice heard by Adam (see Gen. 2:18,20-25).
2. What you hear can bias your mind. Jesus Christ said we should be careful what we listen to. What you hear can interfere with the way you process what you receive spiritually or naturally. Many Christians cannot receive from anointed messengers because of what they heard about the messenger.

EXERCISES

A. Has your mind been tainted by voices that interfere with God's plan for your life?

Discussion

B. Have you interfered with God's plan for another by saying things without direction from God?

Discussion

C. How much credibility do you give to those who gossip or are very opinionated?

Discussion

The Voice of the Devil and His Agents

POINTS TO NOTE

1. The next voice Adam and Eve (humankind) heard was the voice of satan (see Gen. 3:1-5). You can hear the voice of satan in a variety of ways: in an audible voice, he can put ideas into your mind, and he can cause bewitchment (see Gal. 3:1). Satan can cause confusion or blindness to your mind (see John 13:2; 2 Cor. 4:4; 1 Chron. 21:1).
2. Satan's favorite method is destabilizing a person and then penetrating to cause confusion. If he succeeds, then he gradually takes over the person's reasoning faculty.

EXERCISES

A. Have you heard satan's audible voice?

Discussion

B. Has satan polluted your mind with his evil?

Discussion

C. Has satan taken over your ability to reason?

Discussion

The Voice of the Flesh or Self

POINTS TO NOTE

1. The next voice heard was that of the activated soul, the voice of the flesh. This is the echo of your desires, good or bad, including the voice of human logic or the voice of intellectualism. It is the voice of your bodily desires, covetousness, the lust of the eyes and the flesh, and the pride of life (see Gen. 3:9-13).
2. Self-realization made Adam and Eve aware of their nakedness. This is the voice of the flesh, the voice of the human mind. Before this point the Bible says they were naked but they were not ashamed (see Gen. 2:25). They were naked but covered by the glory of God emanating from absolute dependency on God.
3. Unless you deliberately put off the voice of the mind, you cannot hear accurately from God. Your mind, emotions, and desires can play out in your dreams and visions or any other form of revelation. Your natural and spiritual senses can influence how you hear from God; therefore it is important that you know how these senses operate.

EXERCISES

A. How loud is the voice of flesh in your life?

Discussion

B. How loud is the voice of self in your life?

Discussion

C. What do you do to lessen the noise coming from these voices?

Discussion

Strengthen Your Spirit

POINTS TO NOTE

1. You need to strengthen your spirit to receive revelation. Apostle Paul says that humankind is made up of the spirit, soul, and body (see 1 Thess. 5:23).
2. *The strength of your spirit is your capacity to bear witness with the Spirit of God*. You strengthen your spirit by crucifying the flesh, studying the Word of God, and dwelling in the presence of God. Spiritual senses outlive the natural senses. The story of Lazarus and the rich man illustrates this (see Luke 16:19-31).
3. Purposeful application of three functional components of the spirit strengthens the human spirit:

- Divine wisdom (see James 3:17); life application of the Word of God.
- Sanctified conscience (see Heb. 9:14); laying aside personal agendas (see Rom. 12:10).
- Communion with God (see Ps. 91:1 and Rom. 8:16); spending quality time with God.

EXERCISES

A. Is your spirit strong enough to receive revelation?

Discussion

B. Does your spirit have the capacity to bear witness with the Spirit of God?

Discussion

C. Are you committed to the purposeful application of the three components to strengthen your spirit?

Discussion

PRACTICAL PRINCIPLES AND DISCUSSION

CHAPTER 12

Sharpen Your Spiritual Senses

POINTS TO NOTE

1. Spiritual senses are the senses operative from your spirit, also known as the senses of your faith, because your spirit operates by faith. Natural senses are limited in the dimensions of time, space, height, and depth. But there are no limitations when using your pure and unpolluted spiritual senses.
2. The superiority of the spiritual senses is because they can operate in the spiritual *and* in the natural realms. Adam and Eve were dependent solely on their spiritual senses until the point when *"the eyes of both of them were opened, and they realized they were naked"* (Gen 3:7). From that point, the soul of humankind increased, encapsulating the spiritual senses.
3. The Bible teaches us that spiritual exercise is more valuable than physical exercises (see 1 Tim. 4:7-8 TLB).

EXERCISES

A. Imagine a day living in the Garden of Eden with only your spiritual senses guiding you.

Discussion

B. In what way does your soul encapsulate your spiritual senses?

Discussion

C. How can you keep spiritually fit?

Discussion

Your Soul

POINTS TO NOTE

1. Your soul is the non-tangible and immaterial part of you; it is also the relational part. When the *spirit* is strong, it dominates the soul, and when the *body* is strong, it dominates the soul. Therefore, whichever is stronger, spirit or body, controls the soul.
2. The soul and the body together represent *the outer self*. On the other hand, the soul and the human spirit together constitute *the inner self*. A *controlled soul* means your emotions are *controlled*, your mind is *renewed* and *submitted* to God, and your will is *yielded* to God.
3. It is possible to have a weak soul and yet be strong in the spirit. For example, Samson was strong spiritually, being anointed from the womb of his mother as a Nazarite, but he manifested weakness in his soul at the same time, which caused him to fall.
4. The outer self (soul and body) therefore is the sum total of your outward interactive front with the fallen world before gaining the true knowledge of the Triune God. The body and the soul tend to be in mutiny to the Spirit of God; they are contrary (see Gal. 5:17).
5. The outer self must progressively give way to the inner self (soul and spirit) (see 2 Cor. 4:16).

EXERCISES

A. Who is more in control of you? Your inner or outer self?

Discussion

B. What can you do to be more controlled by the spirit, your inner self?

Discussion

C. Are there things about your outer self that you would rather not give up?

Discussion

Put Off the Old Self

POINTS TO NOTE

1. The *old self* refers to a person's pre-Christian ways of life, the totality of life before coming to a true knowledge of God (see Eph. 4:22-24).
2. In your old self, the corrupt, depraved, and fallen nature rules and is the summation of the fallen state of humanity and of humankind's rebellion. The work of your old self leads to defeat, failure, sin, and ultimately death.
3. Unless you repent, there is no alternative in your life but to remain a prisoner of your sinful nature. The Bible says that the works of the flesh include: sexual immorality, impurity and debauchery; idolatry and witchcraft; hatred, discord, jealousy, fits of rage, selfish ambition, dissensions, and factions (see Gal. 5:19-20). And without repentance people are filled with every kind of wickedness, evil, greed and depravity, envy, murder, strife, deceit and malice. They are gossips, slanderers, God haters, insolent, arrogant and boastful; they invent ways of doing evil; they disobey their parents; they are senseless, faithless, heartless, and ruthless (see Rom. 1:24-32).
4. The flesh must be crucified, *"Those who belong to Christ Jesus have crucified the flesh* [sinful nature] *with its passions and desires"* (Gal. 5:24).

EXERCISES

A. Have you come to the complete surrender cited in Ephesians 4:22-24?

Discussion

B. The old self leads to defeat, failure, sin, and ultimately death. Have you discarded your old self?

Discussion

C. Carnality is the combination of the body and soul without the rule of the Spirit of God—have you crucified your old self?

Discussion

Put on Your New Self

POINTS TO NOTE

1. Ephesians 4:23-24 (TLB) says, *"Now your attitudes and thoughts must all be constantly changing for the better. Yes, you must be a new and different person, holy and good. Clothe yourself with this new nature."* Apostle Paul gives you the ways you can put on this new nature or self in Romans 12:1-2 and in Ephesians 4:22-32.

2. Apostle Paul also wrote: *"Since, then, you have been raised with Christ, set your hearts on things above, where Christ is, seated at the right hand of God. Set your minds on things above, not on earthly things. For you died, and your life is now hidden with Christ in God. When Christ, who is your life, appears, then you also will appear with him in glory. Put to death, therefore, whatever belongs to your earthly nature: sexual immorality, impurity, lust, evil desires and greed, which is idolatry. Because of these, the wrath of God is coming. You used to walk in*

these ways, in the life you once lived. But now you must also rid yourselves of all such things as these: anger, rage, malice, slander, and filthy language from your lips. Do not lie to each other, since you have taken off your old self with its practices and have put on the new self, which is being renewed in knowledge in the image of its Creator" (Col. 3:1-10).

3. It is often not easy to know if you have put on the new self. Paul gives guidance on how to ensure you have put on the new self: *"Therefore, as God's chosen people, holy and dearly loved, clothe yourselves with compassion, kindness, humility, gentleness and patience. Bear with each other and forgive one another if any of you has a grievance against someone. Forgive as the Lord forgave you. And over all these virtues put on love, which binds them all together in perfect unity. Let the peace of Christ rule in your hearts, since as members of one body you were called to peace. And be thankful. Let the message of Christ dwell among you richly as you teach and admonish one another with all wisdom through psalms, hymns, and songs from the Spirit, singing to God with gratitude in your hearts. And whatever you do, whether in word or deed, do it all in the name of the Lord Jesus, giving thanks to God the Father through him"* (Col. 3:12-17).

EXERCISES

A. How is your new self being renewed in knowledge in the image of its Creator?

Discussion

B. Are you certain that you have put on your new self?

Discussion

C. Does *the peace of Christ rule in your heart, and the word of Christ dwell in you richly?*

Discussion

God's Peace

POINTS TO NOTE

1. *The peace of God you enjoy determines your maturity in God.* The peace of God is a gift from God that you should jealously guard. Without peace, you may not be able to recall your dreams, and to a lesser extent your visions. This is a common reason why most people do not remember their dreams when they are troubled.
2. *Have a good grip on your thought life.* Your thought life eventually determines who you become. A thought is a seed for the future—what you spend time on, you make room for. Your thought life is reflected in your dreams and visions.
3. *Pay attention to things done at the close of each day.* At the close of each day, spend time meditating on the things of God. This prepares your spiritual soil for whatever nightly encounters God may have for you.
4. Proper application of the revealed truth is influenced by the peace and godly liberty you enjoy. Hence, the presence of the Holy Spirit determines the level of understanding of the revelation and its eventual application.

EXERCISES

A. Do you jealously guard your peace against the devil?

Discussion

B. Do you have a good grip on your thought life?

Discussion

C. Do you pay attention to God at the close of each day?

Discussion

PRACTICAL PRINCIPLES AND DISCUSSION

CHAPTER 13

God's Mysteries

POINTS TO NOTE

1. Your spirit may know something unknown to your mind. There are examples of this in the Bible including Luke 9:45.
2. Another example of this phenomenon is the story of the disciples on the way to Emmaus. The Bible says that God kept the disciples from recognizing Jesus Christ but at the right time, their eyes were opened and they recognized Him (see Luke 23:13-16,30-31).
3. After their eyes were opened and they recognized Jesus Christ they asked each other, *"Were not our hearts greatly moved and burning within us while He was talking with us on the road and as He opened and explained to us [the sense of] the Scriptures?"* (Luke 24:32 AMP). The moment they described their hearts were burning is when they received revelation into their spirits. But only when the Lord broke the bread at the Last Supper were their minds opened to the understanding.
4. Hidden meanings keep you humble and reliant on the Holy Spirit. Although Paul received all revelations from God, to keep him humble, God allowed satan to afflict him with a thorn in his flesh (see 2 Cor. 12:7).

EXERCISES

A. Why do you think the disciples were kept from recognizing Jesus on the road to Emmaus?

Discussion

____

____

____

B. Does your heart burn when you are in the presence of God?

Discussion

____

____

____

C. Remaining humble is an ongoing challenge for most believers. Have you succeeded?

Discussion

A Mystery Is a Truth

POINTS TO NOTE

1. Hidden meanings in your dreams and visions are part of the mysteries of God. *A mystery is a truth that can only be divinely unfolded and is unknowable through reasoning*. You have to be aware of something before you can realize that it is inexplicable. That awareness is the impartation of the mystery in the spirit, but the understanding has to come to the mind.
2. It is the sovereignty of God to decide to whom He will unfold anything mysterious. It is also the prerogative of God to decide when and how much to reveal, where to reveal it, and also why reveal it all (see Deut. 29:29 NLT).
3. When God reveals something, it immediately becomes fruitful (imparted) to the spirit of the recipient. Often the time of reception of the revelation in the spirit may differ from the time appointed for the understanding to come to the mind. This phenomenon is part of what is called *sealed mysteries* in the Bible. Therefore, move in faith and trust that at the right time God will give the fuller understanding (see 1 Cor. 14:14).
4. Many believers are able to survive the things that many others could not because God in His infinite wisdom has endowed their spirits with divine substance through revelatory promises even though they may be unknown to our natural consciousness.

EXERCISES

A. Have you encountered mysteries of God? Were they eventually revealed to you?

Discussion

B. Are you patient enough to wait for the understanding of what is revealed to the spirit to come to the mind?

Discussion

C. Do you agree that you have been able to survive things that others could not because God endowed your spirit with divine substance through revelatory promises even though unknown to your natural consciousness?

Discussion

Why the Secret?

POINTS TO NOTE

1. God may impart your human spirit yet keeps your mind from gaining meaningful understanding of the revelation. There are many reasons, including:
    - To impart your spirit with destiny and yet save you from the "pride of life."
    - To strengthen your spirit to rise to challenges.
    - To save you from the compromising Christian standards and keep you above difficult circumstances.
    - To keep the spirit fervent yet calm so you can wait for other events or people to be ready for their roles in the fulfillment of the destiny; otherwise humans tend to run ahead of God's appointed time.
2. A fascinating example of when God speaks only to the spirit of a person is the story of Elijah and the widow. God clearly told Elijah to go to Zarephath and that He had *commanded* a widow to provide for him. When Elijah arrived, he met the widow but it seemed that she had not received instruction from God; it was unknown to her mind (see 1 Kings 17:8-16). But later actions showed her spirit has been primed or commanded by God.
3. God can prepare you to face certain challenging situations by intimating your spirit with the revelation ahead of the mind realization. Perhaps this helps keep you from undue worries. The "That is that" phenomenon (when God uses a current event to prompt you to a previous impartation in your spirit) is very common; your ability to recognize it and take appropriate action depends on your ability to hear the still small voice of God.

4. God spoke to Samuel the night before he met Saul. When Samuel eventually met Saul, God prompted him (see 1 Sam. 9:15-20). Other scriptural examples include John's experience in Revelation 10:4 (NASB). John was told to stop and seal up the message they spoke. Though we should seek God for revelations and insight, God decides who and when to reveal things. Apostle John was later told not to seal the words of prophecy: *"Do not seal up the words of the prophecy of this book, because the time is near"* (Rev. 22:10).
5. Jesus Christ is the hidden wisdom of the age but destined to be revealed to us (see 1 Cor. 2:6-8). Prophet Daniel had many of these sealed-up experiences as well (see Daniel 8:26; 12:4,9-10).
6. Zechariah and Daniel were mightily used of God in the revelatory realm. In many instances, they relied on an angelic interpreter to help them unfold the scenes with hidden meaning. In other words, to understand all dreams/visions means to possess the humility to seek relentlessly after what might not be clear in the dream. *All you may need is the panoramic view of the dream's meaning and keep on relying on the Holy Spirit to bring more light on your understanding as time progresses.*

EXERCISES

A. Has God ever prepared you to face certain challenging situations by intimating your spirit with the revelation ahead of the mind realization?

Discussion

B. Although we should seek God for revelations and insight, are you patient enough to let God decide who and when to reveal things?

Discussion

C. Do you realize that you need the panoramic view of the dream's meaning and the Holy Spirit to bring more light on your understanding as time progresses?

Discussion

While Waiting

POINTS TO NOTE

1. While waiting for God to unfold the mystery or hidden meaning in dreams:

- Stay humble.
- Be obedient and accountable for what is unfolded to your understanding.
- Remain sensitive.
- Remain in the spirit.
- Seek Him for wisdom.
- Seek His love and who He is.
- Study the Word.
- Do not forsake the assembly of the saints.
- Don't be discouraged.
- Be confident that at the appropriate time God will unfold the mystery.

EXERCISES

A. Which of the reasons cited at the beginning of this section seem the most plausible to you?

Discussion

B. Do you believe that God prepares you ahead of time to face certain challenges by intimating your spirit with the revelation ahead of the mind realization?

Discussion

C. Do you find the mysteries of God to be frustrating, exciting, or confusing?

Discussion

PRACTICAL PRINCIPLES AND DISCUSSION

CHAPTER 14

Dialoguing with God

POINTS TO NOTE

1. Dialoguing with God in dreams is often a series of dreams and the dreamer awakens and intercedes in response to the preceding dream. God then replies to the dreamer's response with another dream and so continues the discussion. This phenomenon is common, but most people miss it thinking they are repeat dreams.

2. I believe that Joseph's dreams were a pair of dialoguing dreams, and God used the second dream to correct the restricted perspectives of Joseph's view of the promised rulership:

   Jacob lived in the land where his father had stayed, the land of Canaan. This is the account of Jacob's family line. Joseph, a young man of seventeen, was tending the flocks with his brothers, the sons of Bilhah and the sons of Zilpah, his father's wives, and he brought their father a bad report about them. Now Israel loved Joseph more than any of his other sons, because he had been born to him in his old age; and he made an ornate robe for him. When his brothers saw that their father loved him more than any of them, they hated him and could not speak a kind word to him. Joseph had a dream, and when he told it to his brothers, they hated him all the more. He said to them, "Listen to this dream I had: We were binding sheaves of grain out in the field when suddenly my sheaf rose and stood upright, while your sheaves gathered around mine and bowed down to it." His brothers said to him, "Do you intend to reign over us? Will you actually rule us?" And they hated him all the more because of his dream and what he had said. Then he had another dream, and he told it to his brothers. "Listen," he said, "I had another dream, and this time the sun and moon and eleven stars were bowing down to me." When he told his father as well as his brothers, his father rebuked him and said, "What is this dream you had? Will your mother and I and your brothers actually come and bow down to the ground before you?" His brothers were jealous of him, but his father kept the matter in mind (Genesis 37:1-11).

3. The following steps will help you dialogue in dream communications. God rewards appropriate responses with further discussion:

   - Ask God for clarification for areas that are not clear in the dream encounter.
   - Have faith that God will hear, respond, and answer.
   - Be sensitive in the spirit to pick answers to questions asked; whether in further dreams or visions or any other form of revelation.
   - Live a life of prayers and intercession.
   - Seek the mercy and grace of God at all times; it is by His grace that you are who you are.

- Seek the wisdom of God at all times by studying the Word of God.
- A life of fasting and sacrifice sharpens your dream life.
- Very importantly you should keep record of your encounters with God.

EXERCISES

A. Have you experienced a series of dreams and have you interceded in response to the preceding dream?

Discussion

B. Knowing what you do now, how would you respond if you received similar dreams to those of Joseph?

Discussion

C. Which of the seven steps do you most agree with? Have the most trouble following?

Discussion

Dream Clues

POINT TO NOTE

1. God leaves clues in dreams to help us unravel the dream's mystery. The following clues may help you understand the meaning of your dreams and initiate dialogue.

    - Any lingering emotion from the dream.

- Anything out of the usual or the expected.
- Inappropriate responses.
- Inappropriate feeling by you or incongruous reaction from other people.
- Dream phrases.
- The setting or background of most scenes in the dream.
- Scenes of confusion or forgetfulness.
- Emotion, pains, joy, fear, etc., in the dream.
- The people in the dream.
- Scenes that portray surprises of either pleasantness or unpleasantness.
- Urgency with which events might have occurred.
- Take note of the concluding emotion that prevailed in the dream or concluding statement when you woke up.

EXERCISES

A. Of the twelve clues, which ones are you most likely to apply to your next dream?

Discussion

B. Do your dreams usually make you feel uneasy or emotionally distraught?

Discussion

C. Do you remember your dream's setting or the people more quickly?

Discussion

The Human Spirit

POINTS TO NOTE

1. From the fallen state to the redemption of humankind, the human spirit exists at two levels: an *unregenerate spirit* and *regenerated spirit*. The regenerated spirit can either be *weak* or *strong*, and the strength of the human spirit determines whether or not you are able to war successfully in the spirit.
2. A weak human spirit is not sustained by power of the Word of God, is not dwelling in the presence of God, and is not being maintained by the constant washing in the blood of Jesus. Hallmarks of a weak spirit include:

- Blurred visions or dreams.
- Unusually docile and poor participating roles in dreams or visions, or lack of righteous firmness during dream encounters.
- Fragmented dreams; dreams remembered only in bits and pieces.
- Prolonged period of inability to recall dreams.
- Poor rendering of dreams and visions; unhelpful or useless for others.

3. Communion with God strengthens and empowers the human spirit and builds up by sanctification the human conscience. The following important steps strengthen the human spirit:

- Studying the Bible; life application of the Word of God is wisdom.
- Praying and fasting; breaks the outer self to allow the spirit to be fully expressed.
- Paying attention to your tithes and offerings opens the window of Heaven for you.
- Spending quality time with God reduces the hardening effect of natural living on emotion, human willpower and mindsets.

EXERCISES

A. Do you have a weak human spirit that is not sustained by power of the Word of God, is not dwelling in the presence of God, and is not being maintained by the constant washing in the blood of Jesus?

Discussion

B. God's wisdom empowers your spirit. Do you readily accept His wise advice?

Discussion

C. Quality time with God reduces the hardening effect of living on emotion, human willpower, and an unhealthy mindset. Are you spending quality time with Him?

Discussion

Progressive Revelation

POINTS TO NOTE

1. God does not reveal the entirety of His heart's plan in a single message or dream. He reveals His plan to you progressively, in ways you can handle at that moment. *Progressive revelation* in dreams and visions can occur in any of the following ways:

   - Further revelation on the subject.
   - Emphasis on another aspect of the subject.
   - New direction on the matter.
   - Confirmation on the subject or part of the subject already revealed.
   - Revealing further progression in relation to the roles of other people.
   - Further progressive revelations through other people, circumstances, or events.

2. Instances of progressive revelations in the Bible include Abraham's first revelation to leave his father's house and move to the land God would show him did not come with much detail (see Gen. 12:1-4). But despite God's economy of words to Abraham, he obeyed God (see Gen. 12:5-6). God furthered His explanation on the subject to Abraham at a later date (see Gen. 12:7-8). God showed a progressive pattern of His revelation to the prophet Daniel. Apostle Paul also received revelations in a progressive manner (see Acts 27:9-11,21-26).

EXERCISES

A. Why doesn't God reveal the totality of His heart's plan in a single message or dream?

Discussion

B. What is a progressive revelation?

Discussion

C. Why is it important to realize that some dreams that might appear as repeat dreams could be progressive revelations on the discourse already begun with God in previous dreams?

Discussion

Spiritual Court Sessions—The Courts of God

POINTS TO NOTE

1. God presides over spiritual court-like sessions, which are not uncommon experiences though many people may not notice them. Judgments from God are fair and balanced perspectives of situations and events because they emanate from God's presence.
2. In this heavenly court, everything is laid bare—even satan's intrigues, craftiness, and schemes are exposed: *"Nothing in all creation is hidden from God's sight. Everything is uncovered and laid bare before the eyes of Him to whom we must give account"* (Heb. 4:13). Examples of this court system are seen in Zechariah chapter 3 and Daniel chapter 7.

3. This court system is all-powerful and towers over the corruptive and manipulative justice system of this perishing world. Biblical examples abound and together with the countless real-life experiences, we see glimpses of a truly divine system that offers clues to how a perfect justice can actually operate.
4. Edicts from these courts with God should not be disregarded because any such violation carries dire consequences. Many people regularly receive court-like audiences with God in their nightly encounters; it is important to know how to truthfully handle these verdicts.

EXERCISES

A. Judgments from the court audiences with God are fair and balanced perspectives that emanate from God's presence and judgment. Are you ready to be judged by The Judge?

Discussion

B. How would a truly divine system of perfect justice operate in an imperfect earth?

Discussion

C. Are you confident that you would handle His verdict correctly?

Discussion

PRACTICAL PRINCIPLES AND DISCUSSION

CHAPTER 15

Dreams or Visions

POINTS TO NOTE

1. Sometimes spiritual experiences are hard to define as either a dream or a vision. It is important to note that some dreams can contain visions and some visions may contain dream experiences. (See Appendix A for a complete list of the different types of dreams and visions.) Examples: a vision in a dream is found in Daniel 7:1; a dream within the context of a vision is found in Genesis 15:12.

2. ***Visions while awake:*** when a vision is experienced by a group of people, commonly the people within the group perceive the vision according to the level of their spiritual visual acuity (the person's visual sharpness) and the sovereign choice of God. The Damascus Road experience is a good example of this circumstance (see Acts 9:1-9). This also happens with most angelic corporal appearances (see Dan. 10:2-9). Sometimes there is full view for all recipients of the corporate vision such as the mysterious handwriting on the wall or other apparitions that can be seen with natural eyes (see Dan. 5:4-6 TLB).

3. ***Dreams while asleep:*** Dreams are only received when asleep and involve only your spirit. Mind and body participation in dream reception is highly restricted. In most cases what appears to be bodily involvement in dream reception is probably because of the visions within the dream.

4. ***Differences between dreams and visions:***

To receive dreams, the mind has to be asleep; see Genesis 15:12-13.	Visions are received with varying degrees of mind alertness.
Dreams are always experienced on a personal basis.	Visions can be experienced in a group setting.
Dreams are received by the spirit of man; are mostly spirit-to-spirit encounters.	Visions may involve varying degrees of the physical or natural realm, such as tangible bodily experiences.
Dreams are more symbolic.	Visions are more literal.

5. In Acts 2:17, the Amplified Bible refers to *vision* as divinely granted appearances and *dreams* as divinely suggested communications. Dreams are more suggested possibilities than inevitabilities. Dreams of promises need to be prayed through for fulfillment. Dreams of warning need to be prayed through so danger can be averted.

6. The writer of Numbers 12:6 indicates that God reveals His divine attributes and He speaks in dreams, which suggests intimacy and a heart-to-heart connection.

EXERCISES

A. Do you experience more dreams or visions? Why do you think that is?

Discussion

B. Do you pray through dreams of promises for fulfillment? Do you pray through dreams of warning to avert danger?

Discussion

C. Do you have a heart-to-heart connection with God through your dreams?

Discussion

Visions

POINTS TO NOTE

1. A vision is the visual reception of revelation or visual perception of a supernatural event—usually perceived by spiritual eyes (see Acts 2:17 AMP). As a Christian you should not seek visions as many non-Christians do. Many do this in the name of "visionary quest." But you should *seek God* realizing that it is through His initiative that spiritual experiences are *divinely granted.*

2. Visions are usually seen with spiritual eyes and encompass a wide spectrum of spiritual occurrences. There is great interplay between the supernatural and natural realms in most visionary encounters. In most cases this is not the same with pure dreams or dreams without visionary components. When a visionary happening permeates the physical realm and becomes perceptible with natural eyes, it is then called an *apparition*.
3. To what degree you perceive a vision depends on God, your giftedness, and your spiritual visual acuity (ability to see into the spirit ream). With well-matured spiritual visual acuity, you can see a vision that others can't. This explains the varying perceptions among people receiving a corporate vision.

EXERCISES

A. Have you experienced a vision in which there was great interplay between the supernatural and natural realms?

Discussion

B. Do you know of any successful visionary quests?

Discussion

C. Have your eyes been opened after someone has prayed for you to see into the spiritual realm?

Discussion

Visionary Appearances

POINTS TO NOTE

1. Visionary appearances can take various forms, including ones with significant auditory perception, such as with young Samuel during his tutelage under Eli (see 1 Sam. 3:15). There are uncommon ones such as the transfiguration of Jesus (see Matt. 17-9). And also life-transforming ones like the one Paul experienced on his way to Damascus.

2. Various forms of visions have been used to call people to action:

- Encouraging visions; Genesis 46:1-5
- Visions with significant auditory component; 1 Samuel 3:10-15
- A call to action; the Macedonian call; Acts 16:6-10
- Warning vision; Acts 18:9. Acts 22:17-21
- Life-transforming vision; Paul's experience on the way to Damascus; Acts 9:3-9
- A call to destiny; Moses' burning bush experience; Exodus 3:1-10
- Visions of divine judgment; the mysterious hand writing on the wall (apparitions); Daniel 5:5-7
- Trances, a twilight state; Acts 10:9-17
- Third heaven experiences; 2 Corinthians 12:1-5

3. Dreams and visions have to be examined within the context of the bigger picture of the interaction between *the earth and the heavens* or between *the supernatural and the natural* realms. Broadly, dreams and visions are the visual perception of the supernatural world from your earthly abode. Visitation of celestial beings to the earth, like angelic visitations, is a way the supernatural world breaks into your earthly world. These occurrences break through the intervening interface called the second heaven.

4. The *second heaven* is the celestial expanse immediately hovering and covering the earth but beneath the *third heaven*. The third heaven is God's abode and home of the departed saints of God. The earth is where we live. An *open heaven* is when the covering of the second heaven over the earth is opened up to establish connection between the earth and the third heaven breaking through the second heaven interface. The third heaven is the highest level of revelatory experience.

EXERCISES

A. Dreams and visions are the visual perceptions of the supernatural world. Have you before considered your dreams as part of the supernatural world?

Discussion

B. Angelic visitations are ways the supernatural world breaks into your earthly world. Have you experienced an angelic visitation?

Discussion

C. How familiar are you with the definitions of these different types of heavens?

Discussion

PRACTICAL PRINCIPLES AND DISCUSSION

CHAPTER 16

The Spiritual Heavenly Realms

Windows, Doors, and Gates of the Third Heaven

POINTS TO NOTE

1. When the third heaven opens, a common manifestation is divine revelation. Other benefits include material and immaterial blessings. The third heaven has doors and windows through which you can access and receive from the spirit realm.
2. The Scriptures speak of the doors, windows, and gates of heaven (see Mal. 3:10 NASB and 2 Kings 7:2). Judgment can also come from the windows of heaven as revealed in Genesis 7:10-14; Revelation 4:1; and Genesis 28:17.
3. The Bible says that the house of God is the gate of heaven. In other words, a good house of God is a good gate of heaven to the people. I believe this is why most people find it easier to gain entrance to the heavenly realm on a corporate basis as we worship in the house of God.
4. Another common manifestation of open heaven is the free flow of the eternal Word of God and availability of the mighty hand of God to perform miracles, wonders, or strange events (see Ezek. 1:1-3).

EXERCISES

A. Have you experienced divine revelation as a result of an opening in the third heaven?

Discussion

B. Do you attend regularly a good house of God that is a good gate of heaven to the people?

Discussion

C. Have you witnessed the free flow of the eternal Word of God and the availability of the mighty hand of God to perform miracles, wonders, or strange events?

Discussion

Visions of the Heavenly Realm

POINTS TO NOTE

1. The interactions between the third heaven and the earth can be grouped into two broad categories—actual and spiritual experiences—and whether it is the third heaven invading the earth or the earth beings experiencing or visiting the third heaven. Every genuine spiritual experience is God's initiative, otherwise it is counterfeit.
2. When God allows humankind to peep into the supernatural realm from the natural realm, these experiences are most of the time spiritual, with a few rare actual experiences. These experiences include:

   - Dreams
   - Visions
   - Translation
   - Throne Room encounters
   - Spiritual experience; Isaiah 6:1
   - Actual experience; 2 Corinthians 12:1-4

   Generally, when the supernatural realm breaks into the natural realm, the experiences are varied and could be either spiritual or actual. Most of these experiences include:

   Apparitions

   - Fourth man in the burning furnace
   - Angelic appearances

Divine sight

- The burning bush experience

Visitation by celestial beings

- Angelic visitations
- Jesus Christ appearing to disciples on the road to Emmaus
- Visitations from the realms of hell

Strange and mysterious events

- The handwriting on the wall
- Wrestling with the angel of the Lord as Jacob did
- Transfiguration of Jesus Christ

EXERCISES

A. Have you accessed the third heaven to receive divine revelations, material and immaterial blessings?

Discussion

B. Has your prayer or worship group or your congregation gained entrance to the heavenly realm on a corporate basis as you worship in the house of God?

Discussion

C. Can you imagine a Throne Room encounter? Describe it.

Discussion

___

___

___

The Third Heaven

POINTS TO NOTE

1. Though invisible, the third heaven is as real and tangible as the earth in which you live. There are constant interactions between the earth and the third heaven, which can be enhanced or clouded. Things you do in the natural world can either hinder or enhance the communication.
2. In Deuteronomy 28:23 it says that *disobedience* to God's commandments can *block* this communication. The opening of the heavens over a person's head is the accessibility of the third heaven to the person on an individual basis through the piercing of the second heaven interface. God can enhance the connection or blanket the communication between the earth and third heaven (see Gen. 28:10-17).
3. Jesus Christ described the essence of New Testament teaching on the concept of open heavens in John 1:49-51. By the death of Jesus, the veil to the most holy place was torn; and by His resurrection, access to the heavens was established. This is without geographical limitations or time restriction! The key requirements are salvation and faith in Jesus; then access to the heavens is granted and built upon Jesus.

EXERCISES

A. Do you believe that the third heaven is as real as the visible and tangible earth in which you live?

Discussion

B. After reading Genesis 28:10-17, how would you describe Jacob's experience?

Discussion

C. Salvation and faith in Jesus opens wide the heavens—have you taken advantage of this access?

Discussion

Heavenly Portals

POINTS TO NOTE

1. An opening of the heavens is bypassing the hindrances of the second heaven to connect the third heaven—God's abode—with the earth. The openness or manifestations of the third heaven over a place can be temporary or permanent. Temporary openness can be periodic or can be accentuated. When the third heaven opens over a place on a permanent basis, it is called a *heavenly portal.*

2. A heavenly portal is a doorway of the third heaven that cuts through the covering of the second heaven and breaks open upon the earth. This doorway is a permanent connection between the first heaven and the third heaven. It originates from God and comes with divine insurance for the permanence of the connection. However, the actions of people and demonic activities can influence the intensity of the traffic at the portal.

3. These portals are usually areas of high spiritual contention between the devil, his cohorts, and godly agents. The Bible is replete with instances of abuse and misuse of these places. Ignorantly, non-Christians have frequently used such portals as places to seek God's power by ungodly means. Others have used portals for visionary quests, idolatry practices, and ritualistic activities. Most high places in the Bible were built on the premise of easy accessibility of the heavenly realm in these places (heavenly portals).
4. At the heavenly portal in Bethel, Jacob's spiritual eyes were opened, and he saw the traffic of angels ascending and descending on a ladder connecting the earth and the third heaven. He also saw God at the heavenly end of the ladder. In this encounter, God conferred Abraham's blessing on Jacob. This all came to Jacob in a dream of the night (see Gen. 28:16-22).
5. The devil always seeks to influence the portal. First, he attempts to possess the traffic on the pathway for his evil watchman activities. Second, he tries to oppress and pollute human activities in this place. Ultimately the devil seeks to establish demonic practices in these places. However, when believers take appropriate steps to move toward God, the portal can become sanctified and consecrated once again to God.

EXERCISES

A. Do you know of heavenly portals? What types of activity are prevalent there?

Discussion

B. How can the devil influence the activity of heavenly portals?

Discussion

C. What steps can believers take to sanctify and consecrate the heavenly portals that have been possessed by the devil?

Discussion

PRACTICAL PRINCIPLES AND DISCUSSION

CHAPTER 17

Receiving Open Heaven Revelations

Prayers and Fasting

POINTS TO NOTE

1. The temporary opening of the third heaven over a location on earth or over your head can be facilitated by what you do, especially prayer and fasting, right standing with God, crying out to God, and your actions and attitude. You can take deliberate actions to enhance the easy flow of divine revelations over a place (see Acts 10:9-11). In this instance, Peter's prayers and fasting undoubtedly contributed to the sudden opening of the heaven upon him.
2. Other examples of temporary openings of heaven:
    - *Right standing with God.* The prophet Ezekiel's right standing with God facilitated the opening of the heavens over him for the following encounter to occur (see Ezek. 1:1). Jesus' obedience and submission to the will of God enhanced the opening of the third heaven over Him (see Matt. 3:16-17).
    - *The cry of the people.* The prophet Isaiah cried out that the Lord would tie open the heavens and come down; the genuine heart cry of the people enhances the openness (see Isa. 64:1).
    - *Actions and attitudes of the people.* At another time, the prophet Isaiah experienced an open heaven that he associated with the year when King Uzziah died. The Bible does not say why Isaiah associated the open heaven with that time; perhaps it was because the kingdom had remarkable success in the infrastructures and the political, agricultural, and military machineries, that the people became spiritually blinded and more reliant on the worldly system rather than the arm of God—who gave the wisdom for the worldly successes (see 2 Chron. 26:7-16). It is possible that when King Uzziah died, there was a significant paradigm shift to begin to rely on the arms of God; as a result there was an enhanced openness of the heavens over Isaiah and people like him (see Isa. 6:1-2).
3. A temporary opening of the heaven over a place can simply be an act of God as we see in Jacob's experience on his way to Haran; the heavens opened upon him, and he saw a vision of a ladder from earth to heaven.

EXERCISES

A. Are you prepared to take the following actions to access blessings from an open heaven: pray and fast, insure right standing with God, cry out to God, take action and have a right attitude?

Discussion

B. What circumstances can you think of that would enhance the openness of the heavens?

Discussion

C. Have you seen a similar scenario as the one cited in Isaiah 6:1-2?

Discussion

Preparing to Receive Revelations

POINTS TO NOTE

1. Over the years, I have experienced both periods of intense revelatory reception and periods when revelations from God are rare. There are also things that can either diminish or increase the ability to receive revelations. The potential to receive is the giftedness, but the quantity and quality of what you receive is dependent on your walk and intimacy with God—God confides in those who fear Him.
2. Let's look at how you can enhance your ability to receive in an open heaven situation.

   - Intimacy with God (see Prov. 3:32 AMP; Ps. 25:14).

- Exercising spiritual senses (see Heb. 5:14).

If you pay attention to what you receive and seek the face of God, you get godly interpretation of your revelations. The more you use your spiritual senses, the sharper the understanding of spiritual things. Good understanding leads to appropriate response. Appropriate response to what God is doing in heaven leads to further release of revelations from Him.

- Being Bible-guided in your spiritual life. As revealed in Deuteronomy, the heavens over a place can become inaccessible if the people live in disobedience to God (see Deut. 28:23).
- Strengthening your spirit (see Eph. 1:17-19).

You are as strong as your spirit is. The strength of your spirit reflects the quality of your relationship with God. A strong spirit receives clearly and abundantly from God. *The strength of the spirit is your ability to bear witness with the Spirit of God.* You can recognize the prompting of God and discern what is godly and what is not.

EXERCISES

A. Can you think of places on earth where the heavens over them are inaccessible because the people are living in disobedience to God?

Discussion

B. You are only as strong as your spirit. How strong are you?

Discussion

C. Are you receiving more revelation because your spirit is bearing proper witness with the Spirit of God?

Discussion

Other Preparation Ingredients

POINTS TO NOTE

1. If you have a good prayer life, you will receive wonderful revelatory encounters with God. Prayer and fasting bring double blessings.

   - You must have a consistent and effective prayer life (see 2 Chron. 7:14; 1 Kings 3:4-5).
   - Fasting breaks the hold of the outer self and allows the inner self to manifest expressly (see Isa. 58:6). Unless the outer self is broken, the inner spirit self will remain unexpressed (see Heb. 9:8). When the inner self is fully manifest, you are better able to receive and relate to God.

2. Giving tithes and offerings brings God's blessings (see Acts 10:2-4). King Solomon's one night encounter in the court of God illustrates this principle very well (see 1 Kings 3:4-5). In the book of Malachi, God said to bring the whole tithe into the store house, so there would be food in His house. Then He said he would open the window of heaven and pour out a blessing until it overflows (see Mal. 3:10 NASB). When the window of heaven is opened, not only physical blessings are released, there is also an increase of revelation from God and enhanced ability to receive from Him.
3. Meditating on the Word of God prepares you for blessings (see 2 Peter 1:19). As the Bible says, the entrance of the Word brings light. When you are well-grounded in the Word of God, revelations will not only increase, revelations will be received with great clarity. Stand firm and hold on to the promises of God until you see the hope of God rise in your heart.
4. Staying in the place of your calling or responsibility will bring His blessings to you (see Luke 2:8-9). Though we are not quite sure why God chose to reveal this great news to these shepherds, we can be sure of one thing, they were at their post of responsibility watching over their flock at night. And while at their post, they received this great revelation.

EXERCISES

A. How are you doing with giving more control to the inner self rather than the outer self?

Discussion

____

____

____

B. The entrance of the Word brings light. Are you standing in the light and are you well-grounded in the Word of God so that revelations will increase and revelations will be received with great clarity?

Discussion

C. Are you willing to stay at your post of responsibility in anticipation of a revelation from God?

Discussion

PRACTICAL PRINCIPLES AND DISCUSSION

Summary

Dreams are important and continue to be relevant to the times we live in—they are far from being obsolete. Dreams are ancient biblical forms of divine communication that need prayerful study and careful application in our present-day living. If God trusted the marriage of Mary and Joseph, the earthly parents of Jesus, and the protection of baby Jesus to a few short and vivid dreams, we ought to take the subject of dreams more seriously.

It was in a vision that the apostle Paul received the Macedonian call and perhaps that was how the gospel spread into Europe at the time it did. Abraham's covenant was consummated in a vision and a dream. Most of the major prophets in biblical days were either called in visions or in dreams; Ezekiel, Isaiah, and the apostle Paul received their call to ministry in dreams or in visions.

The entire book of Revelation is comprised of the visions that the apostle John received while living on the Isle of Patmos. King Abimelek would have lost his life and brought a severe curse upon his people if he had disregarded the advice given to him in a dream. Jacob was given the strategy for economic breakthrough in a dream when he suffered injustice by the hands of his uncle. From Genesis to Revelation and up to our modern times, the importance and relevance of dreams and visions in individuals and the collective destiny of the world cannot be ignored.

In the last days, not only will "old men" dream dreams and "young men" see visions, but also there will be a corresponding release of the spirit of understanding from the very throne of God. God will pour out divine illumination for the understanding of these dreams and visions. Illuminating insights emanating from the very doors of the third heaven will come upon the earth to bring explanation to the mysteries or hidden things of God like never before.

The Bible says, *"The beginning of wisdom is this: Get wisdom. Though it cost all you have, get understanding"* (Prov. 4:7).

It is time to make conscious efforts to leave shallow understanding of our dreams and visions and move into their proper understanding. In this way, we can maximize the benefits of the divine wisdom keys inherent in the dreams that we receive. Imagine, for instance, if Joseph simply told Pharaoh that the meaning of his dream was that something bad was going to happen after a period of a good harvest. (See Genesis 41.) He would have been right, but it would have fallen short of the wisdom keys God intended for the king to have. Yet as I travel around the world I see the prevalence of that type of shallow and partial interpretation everywhere I go. It has to be a lot more than that!

Truly, *"Understanding is a wellspring of life to those who have it..."* (Prov. 16:22 AMP).

PART III

THE PLACE OF SYMBOLS IN OUR REVELATIONS

CHAPTER 18

Biblical Symbols

POINTS TO NOTE

1. Symbols are used throughout the Bible; they are used to represent something or are used to typify something else, either by association, resemblance, or convention. A symbol can also mean a material object used to represent something invisible, such as an idea (the dove as a symbol of peace). A symbol is an image that stands for something but has dual advantage of having its own literal meaning.
2. Symbols may include details you can sometimes find difficult to understand. Patience and due diligence are required to unravel the depth and scope of each symbol's meaning. Only God has the sovereign choice of symbol selection in divine revelation. Because the language of the spirit is rich with symbolism, understanding the symbolic language of God is essential in your walk in the spirit.
3. From the Old to the New Testament, symbols and metaphors were pulled not only from history, but also from the knowledge and culture of the people. In a vision, God showed Ezekiel the valley of dry bones. God explained later that the bones refer to the house of Israel (see Ezek. 37:11). When Jesus Christ said, *"Out of your belly will flow rivers of living water"* (see John 7:38 NASB). He did not mean actual water, but referred to the Holy Spirit.
4. Symbols help you see things from God's perspective because they reflect God's thoughts. Because symbols can have hidden meaning allows God to clarify things in stages, which ensures your dependence on guidance from the Holy Spirit.

EXERCISES

A. Do you have the patience and due diligence required to unravel the depth and scope of each symbol's meaning?

Discussion

B. Do symbols help you see things from God's perspective because they reflect God's thoughts on the matter?

Discussion

C. Does a symbol make you want to search out its meaning while depending solely on the Holy Spirit for guidance?

Discussion

Broaden Your Perspective

POINTS TO NOTE

1. Symbols are used extensively in parables, so symbols and parables are most often linked. A parable is an allegorical representation of something that often embodies a moral or lesson. It is no wonder God uses symbols and parables extensively to speak to you. Symbolism is also the language of the Godhead: God the Father, God the Son, and God the Holy Spirit.

2. Let's look at God the Father. God said of Himself, *"O my people hear My teaching; listen to the words of My mouth. I will open My mouth in parables, I will utter hidden things, things from of old"* (Psalm 78:1-2). He also said, *"I spoke to the prophets, gave them many visions and told parables through them"* (Hosea 12:10).

   But God does not always speak in symbols or parables; He described His pattern of speech to the prophets in Numbers 12:6-8. Lessons from this passage are:

   - God does not speak to everyone the same way.
   - He speaks in dreams and visions.
   - He speaks in clear language.
   - He speaks in riddles or parables.
   - He speaks in dark speeches.
   - He speaks in similitude.

However, you can broaden your perspective if you are open to receive from God in whatever way He may chose to communicate with you. Some people master their dominant way of receiving from God but close the door to other options. This can be tantamount to a tragic error of presumption.

3. Now let us look at God the Son. The teachings of Jesus were full of parables. Jesus taught in parables and used symbols to illustrate His message (see Mark 4:33-34 and Matt. 13:10-13). Just as it was in those days when Jesus taught in parables but explained privately to His disciples, today the parable language of God is available to everyone, but the heathen will "see and hear" without gaining understanding. As Jesus explained the meaning privately to His disciples, so the Holy Spirit explains the meaning of parable language (dreams and visions) to you these days often using the Scriptures.

4. Last, let's look at God the Holy Spirit. The Holy Spirit also speaks in the language that words cannot express (see Rom. 8:26-27). Also, the Holy Spirit helps us understand the spiritual truth in spiritual language (often parable illustration) (see 1 Cor. 2:12-13).

   In summary, God the Father, God the Son, and God the Holy Spirit can speak to you in a variety of ways, including symbolism and parable language. The onus is on you to learn how to decipher these coded messages.

EXERCISES

A. Have you discovered the dominant way that God communicates with you?

   Discussion

B. Have you mastered this dominant way so you can fully receive His messages?

   Discussion

C. Have you kept the door open to receive from God in other ways?

   Discussion

Personal Symbolism

POINTS TO NOTE

1. Through symbolism God brings His message to you individually, relating in you-specific symbolism. A symbol's true meaning can only be revealed to the intended recipient because of the deep individual traits embedded.
2. The language of symbols is deep and powerful; it is the most elementary language and available to all ages. Symbolism also helps with your conceptualization (the ability to form mental imagery). Symbolic thinking helps broaden your different ways of thinking.
3. The following are key points worthy of note (and repeating):

   - To interpret a symbolic revelation you must think symbolically.
   - The choice of symbols in revelations is God's prerogative.
   - Even the most literal revelation may contain some degree of symbolism.
   - As you study the Word of God, you will draw less and less from life experiences and more and more form the biblical reservoir of examples (symbols).
   - Each symbol may have a unique association drawn from your own experience.
   - Symbols are not used haphazardly; their use is specific and purposeful.
   - As symbols are chosen for very specific purposes, it is necessary to first identify what God's purpose is for using a particular symbol.
   - Symbols or symbolic actions come out of the setting of your life, especially your immediate life circumstance.
   - The true meaning of a symbol in a revelation does not come from human reasoning or intellectualism, but by allowing the meaning to flow into your heart or subconscious mind from the Holy Spirit.
   - This flow occurs more easily when you are quiet and still in your heart.
   - A symbolic revelation addresses the issue more frankly than human illustration because the symbolic representation allows emphasis to be placed in the way God sees it.
   - Symbols are not real entities; they are simply representations of the real entities.

EXERCISES

A. It is comforting to know that symbolism keeps the message from being intercepted by the enemy, because a symbol's true meaning can only be revealed to you because of the deep individual traits embedded in symbolic communication.

Discussion

B. The true meaning of a symbol does not come from human reasoning or intellectualism, but by allowing the meaning to flow into your heart or subconscious mind from the Holy Spirit.

Discussion

C. Do you have a constant flow of revelation because you are consistently quiet and still in your heart?

Discussion

PRACTICAL PRINCIPLES AND DISCUSSION

CHAPTER 19

Anatomy of Biblical Dreams

POINT TO NOTE

1. Much can be learned from study of biblical dreams. I have no doubt you will glean wisdom and insight from the following examples: The Dream of the Great Tree, Daniel 4:4-28; The Fulfillment, Daniel 4:28-36; Anatomy of Nebuchadnezzar's Dream of the Large Statue, Daniel 2:31-41.

The Dream of the Great Tree	
Symbol	**Meaning & Symbolic Connotation**
"Stood ***a tree in the middle of the land.*** *...Its height was enormous."*	This is indicative of extensive growth of the kingdom of Babylon. The height of the tree was the sign of the dominion and influence of the kingdom on the world scene.

Anatomy of Nebuchadnezzar's Dream of the Large Statue	
Dream	**Meaning**
An enormous, dazzling statue, awesome in appearance. The head of the statue was made of pure gold. Its chest and arms of silver. Its belly and thighs of bronze. Its legs of iron, its feet partly of iron and partly of baked clay.	The size and appearance of this statue was indicative of what Babylon would become. Babylon was the first of the ancient world powers.

EXERCISES

A. In The Dream of the Great Tree, do you see any other symbolic connotations?

Discussion

B. In reading The Fulfillment passage in Daniel 4:28-36, what meaning do you see?

Discussion

C. In the Anatomy of Nebuchadnezzar's Dream of the Large Statue, has the Holy Spirit given you other meanings to consider?

Discussion

PRACTICAL PRINCIPLES AND DISCUSSION

CHAPTER 20

Symbolic Actions

The following are directly from the *Dictionary of the Prophetic Symbols.* Prayerfully consider each and then complete the exercises.

The Spear of God's Victory	
Symbols	**Meaning/Enactment**
Joshua 8:18 *"...Hold out toward Ai the javelin that is in your hand, for into your hand I will deliver the city...."* Hold out toward Ai the javelin	Joshua 8:19-20 *"As soon as he did this, the men in the ambush rose quickly from their position and rushed forward. They entered the city and captured it and quickly set it on fire. The men of Ai looked back and saw the smoke of the city rising against the sky, but they had no chance to escape in any direction, for the Israelites who had been fleeing toward the desert had turned back against their pursuers."* *"For Joshua did not draw back the hand that held out his javelin until he had destroyed all who lived in Ai"* (Josh. 8:26). Somehow this enactment activated and set in motion certain spiritual forces from God directed to bring defeat to Ai.
A Mighty Angel Acts Out a Prophecy	
Revelation 18:21 *"Then a mighty angel picked up a **boulder the size of a large millstone** and threw it into the sea, and said: 'With such violence the great city of Babylon will be thrown down, never to be found again.'"*	This signifies an "act of God," a mighty force, will be raised up to bring judgment to Babylon and that the force with which the stone touched the water reflects the force with which Babylon will be defeated. Therefore the essence of this prophetic action is to reveal the intensity of the force with which Babylon will be destroyed and the finality of that divine action, just as the stone sank down into the sea never to be seen again.

The Healing of Water	
Symbols	**Meaning/Enactment**
2 Kings 2:19-22 *"...this town is well situated, as you can see, but the water is bad and the land is unproductive.* *a new bowl put salt in it* *threw the salt into it...'I have healed this water....'"*	2 Kings 2:22 *"And the water has remained wholesome to this day, according to the word Elisha had spoken"* A symbolic action enacted by the prophet to break the curse on the city, turning barrenness to fruitfulness. And the water has remained wholesome to this day, according to the word Elisha had spoken. A new bowl = the people need a new and receptive heart of flesh and not the heart of stone Salt in it = allow God to purify their heart and keep it preserved in its pure state, as salt is a purifying and preserving agent. Into the spring = allow the people's hearts to be aligned with the move of God to bring freshness. As the spring reflects the move of God and when purified hearts meet with the move of God, it produces freshness.

Elijah Rebuilt the Altar with 12 Stones	
Symbols	**Meaning/Enactment**
1 Kings 18:30-33 *"...he repaired the altar, which was in ruins.* ***twelve stones,*** *one for each of the tribes descended from Jacob, to whom the word of the Lord had come, saying, 'Your name shall be Israel.' With the stones he built an altar in the name of the Lord...and said, '****fill*** *four large jars with water and* ***pour it*** *on the offering and on the wood.'"*	1 Kings 18:36-39 "At the time of sacrifice, the prophet Elijah stepped forward and prayed: "O Lord, God of Abraham, Isaac and Israel, let it be known today that You are God in Israel and that I am Your servant and have done all these things at Your command. Answer me, O Lord, answer me, so these people will know that You, O Lord, are God, and that You are turning their hearts back again." Then the fire of the Lord fell and burned up the sacrifice, the wood, the stones and the soil, and also licked up the water in the trench. When all the people saw this, they fell prostrate and cried, "The Lord—He is God! The Lord—He is God!"
12 stones	Twelve stones, one for each of the tribes descended from Jacob, to whom the word of the Lord had come, saying, "Your name shall be Israel." A level of unity, predicated on forgiveness and reconciliation that is important before miracles can come from God.
Fill four large jars with water and pour it	Fill four large jars with water and pour it on the offering and on the wood. Statement of faith, because water scarcity. It was also to allow the Spirit of God, symbolized by the water, to take pre-eminence or prevail (the pouring of water on the altar).

Satanic Enactment to Tap Into Counterfeit Power	
Symbols	**Meaning/Enactment**
2 Kings 3:27 *"Then he took his firstborn son, who was to succeed him as king, and offered him as a sacrifice on the city wall...."*	2 Kings 3:27b Powers on the supernatural realm can be accessed by legal or illegal ways. Here the evil king tapped into to evil power in the spirit realm, (the power and authority in the evil realm). The fury against Israel was great; they withdrew and returned to their own land. These counterfeit laws are anti-God in principles and they are largely self-centred, self-exalting, destructive, and inconsiderate of others. These are the laws that regulate the kingdom of darkness.
Israel Defeated the Amalekites	
Exodus 17:8-12 The Amalekites *"I will stand on top of the hill with the staff of God in my hands." ...As long as Moses held up his hands, the Israelites were winning, but whenever he lowered his hands, the Amalekites were winning...."*	Exodus 17:13-16 "So Joshua overcame the Amalekites army with the sword. Then the Lord said to Moses, 'Write this on a scroll as something to be remembered and make sure that Joshua hears it, because I will completely blot out the memory of Amalek from under heaven.' Moses built an altar and called it The Lord is my Banner. He said, 'For hands were lifted up to the throne of the Lord. The Lord will be at war against the Amalekites from generation to generation.'"
I will stand on top of the hill The staff of God in my hands	Top of the hill = the place of prayers/intercession Staff of God = the anointing and mantle of God on his life Hands held up = surrender and total submission to God enacted As long as these conditions were met, Israelites prevailed. When these conditions are not met, the Amalekites gained the upper hand.

Ezekiel 5:1 (Action)	**Ezekiel 5:11-12 (Meaning)**
"Now, son of man, take a sharp sword and use it as a barber's razor to shave your head and your beard..."	Ezekiel was told to take a sharp sword, cut off his hair and beard, and then divide the hair into three parts—each of which symbolized inhabitants of Jerusalem, killed by different methods: • Burning • Striking with the sword • Scattering to the wind • (A few strands were laid aside to represent a remnant, some of whom will also be burned with fire) Shaving the head was an act portraying shame or disgrace in Hebrew culture (see Ezek. 7:18, 2 Sam. 10:4). It also represented a type of pagan practice. Shaving the head was a mark of defilement, making a priest like Ezekiel ritually unclean, and so unable to perform his duties in the temple (see Lev. 21:5). This message was telling the people that they were about to be humiliated and defiled and may not be usable to God.

EXERCISES

A. *"Somehow this enactment activated and set in motion certain spiritual forces from God directed to bring defeat to Ai."* Have you done something in the natural that seems to have had activated things in the spirit and consequences in the natural?

Discussion

B. In the healing of water by the prophet Elijah in Second Kings 2:19-22, what did "new bowl" and "salt" represent?

Discussion

C. In the story of rebuilding the altar in First Kings 18:30-33, what was the significance of the twelve stones?

Discussion

PRACTICAL PRINCIPLES AND DISCUSSION

CHAPTER 21

Symbolic Parables

POINT TO NOTE

1. The parables of Jesus serve two purposes: 1) to reveal truth to believers and 2) to further conceal the truth from those who reject Him or are unbelievers. Positive response is rewarded with further understanding. The following are directly from the *Dictionary of the Prophetic Symbols.* Prayerfully consider each and then complete the exercises.

The Parable of Two Eagles and a Vine (Ezekiel 17)	
Symbols	**Meaning/Enactment**
Ezekiel 17:1-8 *"The word of the Lord came to me: 'Son of man, set forth an allegory and tell the house of Israel a parable. Say to them, "This is what the Sovereign Lord says: A great eagle with powerful wings, long feathers and full plumage of varied colours came to Lebanon. Taking hold of the top of a cedar, he broke off its topmost shoot and carried it away to a land of merchants, where he planted it in a city of traders. He took some of the seed of your land and put it in fertile soil. He planted it like a willow by abundant water, and it sprouted and became a low, spreading vine. Its branches turned toward him, but its roots remained under it. So it became a vine and produced branches and put out leafy boughs. But there was another great eagle with powerful wings and full plumage. The vine now sent out its roots toward him from the plot where it was planted and stretched out its branches to him for water. It had been planted in good soil by abundant water so that it would produce branches, bear fruit and become a splendid vine."*	Ezekiel 17:12-16 *"Say to this rebellious house, 'Do you not know what these things mean?' Say to them: 'The king of Babylon went to Jerusalem and carried off her king and her nobles, bringing them back with him to Babylon. Then he took a member of the royal family and made a treaty with him, putting him under oath. He also carried away the leading men of the land, so that the kingdom would be brought low, unable to rise again, surviving only by keeping his treaty. But the king rebelled against him by sending his envoys to Egypt to get horses and a large army. Will he succeed? Will he who does such things escape? Will he break the treaty and yet escape? As surely as I live,' declares the Sovereign Lord, 'he shall die in Babylon, in the land of the king who put him on the throne, whose oath he despised and whose treaty he broke.'"*

Symbols	Meaning/Enactment
He took some of the seed of your land and put it in fertile soil.	Jerusalem
Another great eagle with powerful wings and full plumage	The king rebelled against the King of Babylon by sending his envoys to Egypt to get horses and a large army. Egypt was a competitive rivalry powerful nation to the Babylonians in the then known world.

Anatomy of the Parable of the Sower

Symbols	Meaning/Enactment
Matthew 13:1-23	
Seed	Word of God; God's promises (something capable of multiplication); something that could be great; offerings, and means of connecting with the future
Soil	Heart of man; potential for multiplication—either good or bad; or the essence of life
Farmer	Jesus Christ, God, pastor, spiritual leaders
"Seed sown along the path" (Matt. 13:19)	No understanding, ungrounded, shallow or poor understanding; easily taken away by the devil or unprotected
a. Along the path b. Birds came c. Ate it up	a. Type of heart b. The work of the devil c. Succumb to the wiles of the evil one
"Seeds fell on rocky places" (Matt. 13:20-21)	Receives the Word with joy, but lacks depth and so easily stolen by trouble and persecution of the world; not rooted; poor foundation. To dream of walking on rocky places is symbolic of times of trouble, persecution, and lack of depth in the matter.

Symbols	Meaning/Enactment
a. Rocky places b. Not much soil c. Sprang up quickly d. Soil was shallow e. Sun came f. They withered g. No root	a. Type of heart that receives the word of God b. Shallow understanding c. Eagerness and joy in receiving the word of God d. Not depth because of poor understanding e. The challenges of life f. Succumb or to be overwhelmed the challenges of life g. Lack of solid foundation and therefore not being properly established in the things of God.
"Seeds fell on thorns" (Matt. 13:22)	The Word of God is heard but choked by worries of life or the attraction of worldly riches. Thorns are symbolic of the worries of life, distraction by worldly riches, or by inordinate ambitions.
a. Thorns b. Thorns grew up c. Choked the plant	a. Worries of life b. The increasing challenges of life c. Worries of life, the desires of the riches of this world create ground not conducive for the Word of God to prosper.
"Seeds on good soil" (Matt. 13:23)	Hears the word, understands and obeys. Therefore becomes fruitful, good state of attitude. Well-prepared for life expectancy, conducive for growth in natural and spiritual things.
a. Good soil b. Produce a crop c. 100, 60, or 30 times what was sown	a. Type of heart b. Productivity c. Different levels of rewards

The Parable of the Weed	
Symbols	**Meaning/Enactment**
Matthew 13:24-30	
A man who sowed	The Son of Man, Teacher, Pastor, the teaching of parents/guardians.
Good seed (wheat)	The sons of the Kingdom—people with good hearts.
in his field	The world, life circumstances
While everyone was sleeping	The most vulnerable time, time of least resistance; time of the weakest defences; the weakest link or point.
The weeds (tares)	The sons of the evil one, people who had no God in their lives
His enemy	The devil, those against the work of God
The harvest	The end of the age, the produce of one's labor
The harvesters	Angels, means by which God brings about our reward.
The kingdom of heaven Why everyone was sleepy It's enemy came Sowed weeds Went away The wheat sprouted and formed ears The weed (tares) also appeared • The owner servant • Fate of the weed (tares) • Fate of the wheat	The good seed in the field. Time of vulnerability. The enemy seizes every opportunity at the time of weakness. To sow thoughts or ideas not of God in the lives of God's people. Camouflage the deception of the devil When the people of the kingdom blossom, the weed also blossomed • Servants of God • Burnt in Hell • Kept in the barns

Symbols	Meaning/Enactment
Matthew 13:36-43	
Tares closely resemble wheat but are poisonous to humans. They are indistinguishable from wheat until the final fruit appears. Thereafter, the farmer would weed out tares just before the wheat is harvested.	The parable of the tares teaches that until Jesus Christ returns—both genuine believers and counterfeits will be allowed to coexist. There will be a period or an age in which the good and the evil remain together, but in the end, the two groups shall be separated.
The Parable of the Mustard Seed	
Matthew 13:31-42	
A mustard seed is a small seed capable of enormous multiplications.	The parable of the mustard seed teaches that although the kingdom may have small numbers of people at the beginning of age, it will ultimately be large and prosperous. Here the birds of air are not evil. Note that in this parable, the birds of the air are not symbols of evil as they were in the parable of the sower.
The Parable of the Yeast and Bread	
Matthew 13:33	
Though in general, leaven in the Scriptures often represents evil, the leaven in this parable could not possibly mean evil.	This parable is pivoted on the picture of the dynamic character of yeast that once it starts, it is impossible to stop, the picture shows that numerical growth will take place—rather not from the power of an external force but will grow from internal dynamic of the working of Holy Spirit. In reality, in the world today, the growth of Christendom is doubling each succeeding generation.

The Parable of the Hidden Treasure	
Matthew 13:44	
The parable teaches values and responsibilities.	The ground to this teaching is that the disciples were forced to count cost contrary to their expectation of a great kingdom; but this parable teaches that despite immediate pressures of earthly problems, the immense value of the kingdom far outweighs any sacrifice of inconvenience that one might encounter on earth to possess it. It is each person's responsibility to try to pay the price and possess it.
The Parable of the Pearl	
Matthew 13:45	
The parable teaches that the person finds the pearl not by accident but by diligent search.	Jesus' desire here was to imbue them with a high sense of calling to the Kingdom of God. Though salvation is by faith, ultimately it is a choice that one has to make at an individual level.
The Parable of the Net	
Matthew 13:47-52	
Teaching on the need to lay a large enough net to gather a great number of all kinds of fish without discrimination.	The job of judging or ferreting out the false catch belongs to God at the end of the age; believers are not equipped to do this. Spread the Word and the gospel to all nations, all races, all people or hearts.

The Parable of the Workers in the Vineyard	
Matthew 20:1-16	
This parable teaches about the redemption of time for the righteous who continue to stand in faith to the end.	The Lord/the Kingdom of God
Vineyard owner: • Early workers • Agreed to pay them a denarius for a day • The other workers (the late comers to the vineyard) • Paid them all the same wages	• The Jews to whom belong the ancestry of Jesus, the promises/covenant (see Rom. 3:1-2; 9:4-6). • the promises/covenant • The Gentiles who will come into some covenant (see Eph. 2:11-13). • Through faith in Jesus Christ, salvation becomes available to all (see Rom. 11:16-17).
The Parable of the Lost Sheep	
Matthew 18:10-14	
This parable teaches that it is not the wish of God that any should perish but that all would come to the knowledge of Him.	
1. A man owns a hundred sheep.	1. Father in Heaven, the Lord owns the earth and the fullness thereof.
2. One of them wanders away.	2. Lost soul, those who fall occasionally, backslider.
3. Look for the one that wandered off.	3. Not willing that any of these little ones should be lost. God's wish that none should perish.
4. He is happier about that one sheep than about the ninety-nine that did not wander off.	4. There is rejoicing in Heaven over a lost soul who is saved. Jesus said He came not for those who are well but those who are sick.

EXERCISES

A. What is an allegory?

Discussion

B. In Ezekiel 17 1-8, what did the "great eagle" symbolize?

Discussion

C. In Matthew 13:24-30, what did the "good seed" symbolize? What did "the weed" symbolize? And what did the "harvesters" symbolize?

Discussion

PRACTICAL PRINCIPLES AND DISCUSSION

CHAPTER 22

Prophetic Acts and Drama
The Power—and Danger

Recognizing True, False, and Satanic Mimicry

POINTS TO NOTE

1. A prophetic act is an act, deed, or mission inspired by the Holy Spirit to bring or facilitate a specific agenda of Heaven on earth. It carries much more results or implications than mere physical action. *Prophetic acting establishes spiritual authority in the invisible realm by means of visible physical action with or without pronouncements*. Prophetic acts take different forms ranging from a simple action to a complex drama that may be difficult for humans to completely comprehend. Prophetic actions are akin to symbolic actions but carry a prophetic message and facilitate a specific heavenly agenda on earth.
2. Prophetic acting and drama are common practices these days. Many are inspired by the Holy Spirit to carry out these acts without necessarily knowing why. Others mimic what they have seen others do. Prophetic acting can carry very significant spiritual powers and consequences that need to be properly understood and harnessed.
3. To be successful, the prophetic act should:
    - Be *inspired and guided* by the Holy Spirit.
    - Be carried out in faith—without faith, it is impossible to please God.
    - Come with *specific instructions for the action to be undertaken,* and strictly adhere to the instructions.
4. The following are important points about prophetic acting:
    - Prophetic acts can open both the physical and the supernatural realms and also open the person performing the act to the power and authority in the spirit realm whether demonic or godly.
    - Prophetic acts can also mean acting out a word of promise or revelation as though already fulfilled in the physical realm, or the act of applying action to prophecy or word of revelation before its fulfillment.
    - Prophetic acts have roots from ancient times. This is what God said in the Book of Hosea: *"I have also spoken to [you by] the prophets, and I have multiplied visions [for you] and [have appealed to you] through* ***parables acted out by the prophets*** (Hosea 12:10 AMP).

- A true prophetic act can be enacted out by human beings or by a celestial being, but it is always under the inspiration of the Spirit of God.

EXERCISES

A. "A prophetic act is an act, deed, or mission inspired by the Holy Spirit to bring or facilitate a specific agenda of Heaven on earth." Write this definition in your own words and use personal experiences in your definition.

Discussion

B. *"And so it was, when Moses held up his hand, that Israel prevailed; and when he let down his hand, Amalek prevailed"* (Exod. 17:11). List two other biblical instances of a prophetic act being played out.

Discussion

C. Have you or someone you know been led by the Holy Spirit to carry out prophetic acts without knowing why? Did you eventually discover the reason?

Discussion

POINTS TO NOTE

1. **Spontaneous Common Physical Actions**

Many spontaneous common physical actions that often carry far-reaching spiritual implications include:

> ***Dancing and Leaping***. *"Let them praise His name with dancing and make music to Him with tambourine and harp"* (Psalm 149:3).

Lifting Hands and Bowing Heads. *"Ezra praised the Lord, the great God; and all the people lifted their hands and responded, 'Amen! Amen!' Then they bowed down and worshiped the Lord with their faces to the ground"* (Nehemiah 8:6).

Groaning in Prayer. *"Not only so, but we ourselves, who have the firstfruits of the Spirit, groan inwardly as we wait eagerly for our adoption as sons, the redemption of our bodies"* (Romans 8:23). *"My dear children, for whom I am again in the pains of childbirth until Christ is formed in you"* (Galatians 4:19).

Shaking or Trembling. *"The jailer called for lights, rushed in and fell trembling before Paul and Silas"* (Acts 16:29).

"The sight was so terrifying that Moses said, 'I am trembling with fear'" (Hebrews 12:21).

Intense Weeping. *"No one could distinguish the sound of the shouts of joy from the sound of weeping, because the people made so much noise. And the sound was heard far away"* (Ezra 3:13).

2. **Prophetic Acts**

A prophetic act can be performed during the following conditions:

Intercession

By a prophetic act of sacrificing to the God of the Hebrews, the prophet Samuel interceded for Israel, and the heavens fought on behalf of the Israelites (see 1 Sam. 7:10-13). This is also a prophetic act by blood sacrifice.

Prayers

King Hezekiah's humble act of trusting God in prayers (see 2 Kings 19:14-20). The Lord heard King Hezekiah's plea (see 2 Kings 19:35-37).

Spiritual Warfare

After the defeat of the walled city of Jericho, the Israelites suffered humiliating defeat by the hands of the relatively small city of Ai. When Israel made atonement for their sin, God asked Joshua to performed a prophetic act and they were then able to overtake the city of Ai. God told Joshua to perform a prophetic act in order to facilitate the victory over the City of Ai (see Josh. 8:18-19,26). Joshua performed another symbolic action prophetically (see Josh. 10:22-26).

Dramatization of Divine Message

The prophet Ahijah launched a dramatic prophetic act signaling God's approval of Jeroboam's rule in Israel. When Jeroboam, then an official at King Solomon's palace, was on his way to Jerusalem, the prophet Ahijah met him and dramatized his message from God to Jeroboam (see 1 Kings 11:29-31; 12:15-16).

Impartation of Blessing

By prayers and prophetic action, Jacob blessed the sons of Joseph and Ephraim ahead of Manasseh (see Gen. 48:10-20).

Proclamation of a Curse

The prophet Jeremiah used prophetic action to issue a curse on Babylon (see Jer. 51:60-64).

Deliverance from a Curse

The city of Jericho was suffering under burden of curse, but the men of the city came to the prophet and he performed a prophetic act and the curse was reversed and the city was delivered from the curse (see 2 Kings 2:19-22).

EXERCISES

A. Have you witnessed or personally experienced spontaneous common physical actions such as the five mentioned? What were the circumstances surrounding the experience?

Discussion

B. In today's church environment, is it most common for a prophetic act to be performed during intercession, prayer, spiritual warfare, dramatization of a divine message, impartation of a blessing, or proclamation of or deliverance from a curse?

Discussion

C. What does dramatizing a message from God mean to you?

Discussion

Carrying Out a Prophetic Act

POINTS TO NOTE

1. The following two conditions are important in carrying out a prophetic act: 1) the need for strict adherence to the instructions and 2) the need for continuous alertness in the spirit. When Elisha the prophet was on his dying bed and before his last breath, he performed a prophetic act in intercession on behalf of Israel (see 2 Kings 13:14-19). Later this prophecy was fulfilled and led to King Jehoash receiving the justice of God (see 2 Kings 13:24-25). In the midst of an anointed presence, ordinary acts can assume prophetic significance such as in the story of Saul when he tore the prophet Samuel's garment. The prophet said it was symbolic of the way the kingdom will torn away from Saul (see 1 Sam. 15:27-28).
2. Avoid disobedience or irreverence to God during prophetic acting. The story of Moses and his staff is an example of what to avoid during prophetic acting (see Num. 20:7-10). Moses failed to follow strict instruction: *"Then Moses raised his arm and struck the rock twice with his staff. Water gushed out, and the community and their livestock drank"* (Num. 20:11). His punishment was costly, perhaps, to whom much is given much is required (see Luke 12:48). Because of his disobedience, Moses did not enter the Promised Land (see Num. 20:12).
3. A false prophetic act is acting out a word or an idea without the inspiration of the Spirit of God and can be initiated by selfish agendas with the intent to cause deception (see Jer. 28:10-17). Even though the most common false prophetic acts are usually based on presumption with no deception intended, they also attract rebukes from God. God rebuked Job's presumptuous friends, *"After the Lord had said these things to Job, he said to Eliphaz the Temanite, 'I am angry with you and your two friends, because you have not spoken of me what is right...'"* (Job 42:7). False prophetic acts are capable of exposing a person to the power of the dark side of this world—and often lead to demonic entanglement, delusion, and harmful effects.
4. Even celestial beings carried out prophetic acts in order to dramatize the overthrow of violence in the notorious city of Babylon: *"Then a mighty angel picked up a boulder the size of a large millstone and threw it into the sea, and said: 'With such violence the great city of Babylon will be thrown down, never to be found again'"* (Rev. 18:21).

EXERCISES

A. Why do you think the two conditions in carrying out a prophetic act—1) the need for strict adherence to the instructions and 2) the need for continuous alertness in the spirit—are so important?

Discussion

______

______

______

B. Have you or do you know someone who has been rebuked by God for disobedience or irreverence during prophetic acting?

Discussion

C. Have you or do you know someone who has been exposed to dark, satanic forces because of a false prophetic act?

Discussion

Recognizing Satanic Mimicry of Prophetic Acts

POINTS TO NOTE

1. The satanic equivalent of prophetic acts, evil enactment, is the satanic counterfeit of prophetic acts and actions inspired by the devil or his cohorts. These enactments can easily lead to contact with evil spiritual powers. Idol worshiping and demonic incantations are common examples of this practice (see Ezek. 8:16).
2. A biblical example of demonic mimicry of prophetic acting: *"When the king of Moab saw that the battle had gone against him, he took with him seven hundred swordsmen to break through to the king of Edom, but they failed. Then he took his firstborn son, who was to succeed him as king, and offered him as a sacrifice on the city wall. The fury against Israel was great; they withdrew and returned to their own land"* (2 Kings 3:26-27). The descendants of Moab became neighbors of the Israelites. Over time, the Moabites became subjugated to Israel and had to pay tributes. When King Mesha rebelled against Israel, the kings of Judah and Edom allied with Israel against Moab. The tide of the battle went seriously against the Moabites. To Mesha, if they were defeated in the battle, it meant only one thing—his god Chemosh was angry with Moab. Consequently, Mesha offered his son, heir to the throne, to his god. The Israelites were disgusted and pulled off their attack.

EXERCISES

A. Have you witnessed an evil enactment—the satanic counterfeit of prophetic acts and actions inspired by the devil or his cohorts?

Discussion

B. How serious to God is idol worshiping and demonic incantations according to Ezekiel 8:16? (See also Deuteronomy 29:17-18, Second Kings 17:17, Second Chronicles 33:6.)

Discussion

C. List two more biblical examples of an evil enactment.

Discussion

What to Avoid as Christians

POINTS TO NOTE

1. Christians must make conscious efforts to avoid evil mimicries because of the possibility of leading to the dark side and the dire consequences. This power can be very alluring but can delude and lead to crippling bondage.

2. Christians should avoid any form of enactment not inspired by the Holy Spirit. Some may appear to be innocuous; but they are not Christian and could be outright demonic. Unchristian enactments include the following that have no biblical basis or inspiration by the Holy Spirit:

- Writing another person's name on a piece of paper and then burning it, hoping to bring judgment upon that person.
- Writing someone's name on a piece of paper and then writing their own name beside it, hoping to invoke love and bonding.
- Physically standing on a Bible to make a pronouncement, thinking it will carry more power. In reality, the power of proclamation rests in the right standing of the proclaimer with God and on whether the proclamation lines up with the will of God.

Evaluate a Prophetic Act before Carrying it Out

POINTS TO NOTE

1. A Christian should not be afraid to carry out an act if prompted by the Holy Spirit. If in doubt, put the act to the following tests:

- Does it speak of the love of God?
- Does it draw you closer to God?
- Does it enhance the Christ-likeness in you?
- Would Jesus do it?
- Does it stir self-exaltation?
- Does it respect human life, even the life of your enemy?

2. The power of prophetic acts includes:

- Settling things in the spirit realm before they manifest in the natural realm.
- Quickening the fulfillment of prophecy.
- Putting action to a word or revelation to break the inertia in unfulfilled promises.
- Acting as momentum to propel spiritual forces.
- Increasing people's faith.
- Empowering angelic beings to act on behalf of the saints.

3. There are many prophetic acts in the Bible. Two examples are the prophetic acts by Nehemiah (see Neh. 5:10-13) and Agabus (see Acts 21:8-14). Many biblical prophets, like Elisha and Zechariah, performed outstanding prophetic acts to facilitate the agenda of Heaven on earth. God directed Zechariah to perform three specific prophetic mimicries/acts as messages to Israel.

Mimicry/Act	Scripture Reference
Signifying that God is **withdrawing favor or grace** from them	**Zechariah 11:7-11** *So I pastured the flock marked for slaughter, particularly the oppressed of the flock. Then I took two staffs and called one **Favor** and the other **Union**, and I pastured the flock. In one month I got rid of the three shepherds. The flock detested me, and I grew weary of them and said, "I will not be your shepherd. Let the dying die, and the perishing perish. Let those who are left eat one another's flesh." Then I took my staff called Favor and broke it, revoking the covenant I had made with all the nations. It was revoked on that day, and so the afflicted of the flock who were watching me knew it was the word of the Lord.*
The **bond of unity** between Judah and Israel is **broken**	**Zechariah 11:14** *Then I broke my second staff called **Union**, breaking the brotherhood between Judah and Israel.*
Illustrating the role of the **worthless, wicked shepherds** in Israel	**Zechariah 11:15-17** *Then the Lord said to me, "Take again the equipment of a foolish shepherd. For I am going to raise up a shepherd over the land who will not care for the lost, or seek the young, or heal the injured, or feed the healthy, but will eat the meat of the choice sheep, tearing off their hoofs. "Woe to **the worthless shepherd**, who deserts the flock! May the sword strike his arm and his right eye! May his arm be completely withered, his right eye totally blinded!"*

4. There are also declarations: *"Thou shalt also decree a thing, and it shall be established unto thee..."* (Job 22:28 KJV).

    - The Lord is my victory, no matter the strength of the enemy who rises up against me; He will help me come out on top every time. *"All the nations surrounded me, but in the name of the Lord I cut them off. They surrounded me on every side, but in the name of the Lord I cut them off. They swarmed around me like bees, but they died out as quickly as burning thorns; in the name of the Lord I cut them off"* (Psalm 118:10-12; see also Psalm 84:11). *"The Lord will make you the head, not the tail. If you pay attention to the commands of the Lord your God that I give you this day and carefully follow them, you will always be at the top, never at the bottom"* (Deuteronomy 28:13).
    - God will meet all my needs according His riches in glory by Christ Jesus and He will watch over me to perform His words concerning me. *"And my God will meet all your needs according to His glorious riches in Christ Jesus"* (Philippians 4:19). *"The Lord said to me, 'You have seen correctly, for I am watching to see that My word is fulfilled'"* (Jeremiah 1:12).

EXERCISES

A. Have you or do you know people who have performed unchristian acts such as mentioned in this section? Can you name other acts that are not satanic yet performed by Christians?

Discussion

B. Prophetic acts are powerful—of the six aspects stated, which three would you say are the most powerful and life-changing?

Discussion

C. Write your understanding of Zechariah 11:7-17.

Discussion

PRACTICAL PRINCIPLES AND DISCUSSION

PART IV

THE WATCHERS OF OUR TIME

CHAPTER 23

Seers, Prophets, and the Watchman Ministry

POINTS TO NOTE

1. Seers are gifted with visions, dreams, and other picture revelations on a consistent basis. They operate mainly from the receptive dimension of the prophetic ministry. A majority of *high volume dreamers* are seers; they usually have long and vivid visions. A *major distinguishing feature* in the ministry of a seer is the occurrence of "strange spiritual experiences" and angelic interactions.
2. The ministry of the watchmen can be regarded as an offshoot of the seer's anointing. Most watchmen are seers (some watchmen operate predominantly from a non-seer dimension). The following are some of the cardinal roles of the spiritual watchman:

- Watching and looking into the distance, especially to see approaching danger.
- Warning those who are endangered.
- Encouraging those who are righteous to continue in their righteousness.
- Warn the wicked to turn from their wickedness.
- Preparing people to give the appropriate protocol to the coming King and His divine messengers.

3. Being a spiritual watchman is to be endowed by God to see things from afar. Therefore, this ministry is a conspicuous target and attracts the fury of the enemy.
4. The ministry of the watchman in a local church is one of the most common yet one of the most misunderstood ministries in the Body of Christ. Many gifted people have been driven into reclusive lives because of relational issues they grapple with within the local church. *Valuable time, resources, and knowledge have been wasted because of wrongly packaged warnings from true but immature watchmen*.
5. There is a growing need for proper training, acceptance, and integration of watchmen. Most local leaderships do not know how to handle watchmen who claim to receive the near-endless visionary revelations—especially when they fail to see the plank in their own eyes.

EXERCISES

A. Who are watchmen? Are you a watchman?

Discussion

B. How best can you be trained, appreciated, and integrated into the Body of Christ?

Discussion

C. How can your potential be channeled as a valuable resource to the local leadership?

Discussion

The Seer's Anointing

POINTS TO NOTE

1. The downside of the seer's anointing is the easy susceptibility to failure in relational issues, the lusts of the eyes, and failure to act on revelation. Giving in to these temptations can make revelations in the seer's realm cloudy, smeared, jumbled, and filled with distorted images. Keeping the seer's character righteous and living a life of continuous sanctification enables the seer to see more clearly.
2. A seer (Hebrew: *ro'eh)* sees visions and dreams consistently; a seer perceives, looks, discerns, or stares into the supernatural to receive revelation mostly by pictures. A seer is divinely enabled to see or discern the will of God, one whose eyes have been divinely unveiled to see and understand things not open to the ordinary person (see 1 Sam. 9:9).

3. The verse in First Samuel does not mean that the term *prophet* has replaced the term *seer*. The term *seer* was more broadly applied in ancient times by the Jewish people. By the time of King David, the term *seer* had narrowed into its exact specifics and the office of the seer and that of the prophet were well-established and distinct:

   He stationed the Levites in the temple of the Lord with cymbals, harps and lyres in the way prescribed by David and ***Gad the king's seer and Nathan the prophet;*** *this was commanded by the Lord through His prophets* (2 Chronicles 29:25).

   King Hezekiah and his officials ordered the Levites to praise the Lord with the words of ***David and of Asaph the seer****. So they sang praises with gladness and bowed their heads and worshiped* (2 Chronicles 29:30).

4. The *nabi* (meaning spokesman) prophet receives mainly by hearing things in the spirit realm. The Hebrew word *naba* means to prophesy and a *nabi* prophet is one who speaks out or is a proclaimer of the will of God (one who speaks by divine inspiration).

   This is a simplistic categorization meant to help rather than restrict. You may find it hard to know which category you fit into. The main help I find in this categorization is that it reassures those in training that gifting may differ, and therefore helps remove frustration. You may find it easy to grow in how to receive divine inspiration by faith without visual signals; whereas for others this may not come easily if they are essentially seers. Remember that there are many who receive, or walk, in both categories or offices. Perhaps the prophet Gad moved in both realms (see 2 Sam. 24:11-12).

5. I believe that the prophet Zechariah operated effectively in both offices. In the beginning of the book of Zechariah, the prophet received eight symbolic visions with significant angelic interaction as messages for the Jewish returnees (chapters 1 to 5), whereas in chapters 6 to 12, the prophet operated mainly as a *nabi* prophet.

EXERCISES

A. Do you consider yourself a seer who is divinely enabled to see or discern the will of God and to understand things that are not open to the ordinary person?

SEER	NABI PROPHET
The seer is gifted with visual revelations on a consistent basis; Gad, Iddo, Hanani and Asap were seers. A seer is characterized by consistent and persistent visual revelation, the experiencing of strange spiritual events, and having common angelic involvement. Seers see events in the supernatural realm before they happen in the natural. Seers more often see and describe. In describing what is seen, some seers grope for vocabulary. The seer's vocabulary capacity affects his ability to express what is received. Ezekiel and the apostle John relied on the capacity of their vocabulary to express what they saw. So on some occasions, seers gave different descriptions to somewhat similar pictorial revelations. Seers are those gifted with visions and dreams on a consistent basis. Also long and vivid visions are common with the seer's anointing. A key distinguishing feature is that the ministry of a seer is characterized by angelic interactions and strange spiritual encounters. On the downside of the seer's anointing is the easy susceptibility to failure in relational issues, the lusts of the eyes, and failure to act on revelation. These are snares to the anointing and functions of the seer's ministry. Giving in to these temptations, particularly those involving the eyes, can make revelations in the seer's realm cloudy, smeared, and jumbled, and filled with distorted images. Most seers need to work on relations with people; some have unfortunately ended up becoming reclusive because of relational issues. Working on the seer's character and a life of sanctification enable the seer to see more clearly. Not all those who receive visual revelation are seers, as visual revelations may be evoked through intensive purification (fasting and prayers) and intercession. The seer's anointing is very sensitive, as seers tend to pick up much visual revelation that leaves long lingering effects. A seasoned seer is adept in the understanding of the dark speeches or mysteries of God because of the frequent search to gain understanding of parables in picture revelations. Seers are often deep thinkers, hence many people describe the seer anointing as the receptive dimension of the prophetic ministry. Because of the reflective nature of the seer's anointing, the well-integrated seer soon becomes a great resource for other prophets. Seers can often become good teachers and administrators as exemplified by the lives of Samuel, Joseph, and Daniel. However, some seers need to put forth much effort to have effective relationships with other people. Some may even become reclusive.	The *nabi* prophet hears and speaks more than he sees and describes. The prophet Isaiah spoke of many future events as he heard them in the spirit realm, hence he was not too reliant on his personality. By faith, a *nabi* prophet receives divine inspirations that bubble to from within him. Most *nabi* prophets get more inspiration once they have started to speak. So they might start slowly but soon bubble into great speed and volume. A *nabi* prophet can prophesy upon many people at a time. They are good exhorters and are often greatly used by God to bring inspiration or motivation to people in moments of despair. They may give general or very specific messages. On the down side, they tend to be extroverts and therefore should make efforts to avoid exaggerations that may give false hope or unattainable expectations.

Discussion

B. Have you become reclusive because of relational issues due to being a seer?

Discussion

C. Do you understand the difference between a seer and a prophet? How about a *nabi* prophet?

Discussion

The Prophet Dreamer

POINTS TO NOTE

1. Prophet dreamers are gifts to the church, and their ability to receive from God is the gift to the prophet. So dreamers need to understand and take care of their gifts before they can become effective gifts to the church.
2. Your gift is not a reward. Credibility is earned. Seasons in dreaming are mainly connected with divine favor and some human factors. Favor with God comes at the point of your call. Favor with people comes at the point of commission. Favor with God facilitates the training, and favor with people allows the manifestation of the anointing.
3. Every prophet dreamer is unique: other people's experience is only a guide.
4. God does not reveal the totality of His message at one time. Revelation is progressive and comes in bits and pieces. You may receive the end before the middle part.
5. Prophetic dream is about the glory of God—not you. Identify your prophetic slant, and your uniqueness will make way for you!

EXERCISES

A. Do you consider yourself a prophet dreamer? Why or why not?

Discussion

B. Do you have the favor of people and God?

Discussion

C. Have you been frustrated because you have not received the total message or revelation? Are you impatient with God?

Discussion

PRACTICAL PRINCIPLES AND DISCUSSION

CHAPTER 24

Angels, Prophecy, and Silence

POINTS TO NOTE

1. *Angels are common in the ministry of the seer* and may include a great deal of angelic interaction. We see this in the ministry of Joseph, the earthly father of Jesus Christ, the apostle John, and the prophet Zechariah (see Zech. 4:1-6).
2. A seasoned seer is more likely to give planned and rehearsed prophecies because the revelations often come in advance of proclamation. Consequently, seers are less prone to errors of presumption, which can be common with spontaneous prophetic utterance. *Generally, it is a misconception that the majority of prophecies are spontaneous*. A good proportion of prophecies are planned and rehearsed, as exemplified by many instances in the Bible. However, these phenomena of planned and rehearsed prophecies are more common in a seer's ministry than in the ministry of *nabi* prophets.
3. Planned prophecies are often remarkably accurate, wise, and relevant. The Bible records a very detailed prophecy given by Samuel, a notable seer in the Scriptures (see 1 Sam. 10:1-10). It is not uncommon that the seasoned seer readily becomes a great support to other prophetic people, as most seers can easily become gifted prophetic teachers. Trances, divine visitations, translations, and Throne Room experiences are common with seers.

EXERCISES

A. Do you frequently have dreams involving unknown persons—angels?

Discussion

B. Have you given planned and rehearsed prophecies purely because revelations often come in advance of the proclamation?

Discussion

C. What stands out the most to you after reading First Samuel 10:1-10?

Discussion

Angelic Involvement

POINTS TO NOTE

1. The Bible is full of dreams involving angels. Although most dreamers have encountered angels in their dreams, they don't actually realize it. The majority of unknown people in your dreams who were trustworthy, helpful, and protective (and not contrary to divine principles) are usually angels concealed in human form. More commonly, a faceless personality in your dreams may refer to the Holy Spirit. (However, an unknown person who is deceptive, untrustworthy, unreliable, and causes hindrance in a dream is evil and symbolic of a demonic spirit.)
2. Angels are common in twilight dreams and are often associated with clear dream phrases that give unambiguous instructions. Angels may bring interpretation in dreams. These interpretations can come in numerous forms, but are usually literal. Remember, however, that the Bible says, *"But even if we or an angel from heaven should preach a gospel other than the one we preached to you, let him be eternally condemned"* (Gal. 1:8). Most interpretations received in dreams need further study, so you should ask God for understanding.
3. Most of the time, angels bring interpretation to us in dreams: see Daniel 7:15-16; Daniel 8:15-16; Zechariah 1:9-10; Zechariah 2:2-6.
4. Angels can wake us up to recall and record our dream: see Zechariah 4:1-3; Daniel 10:7-11.
5. Angels bring impartation in dreams: see Revelation 10:8-11; Luke 1:26-35.
6. Angels bring knowledge in dreams or visions: see Daniel 10:12-14.

EXERCISES

A. Do you believe that you have encountered angels in your dreams but weren't aware of them at the time?

Discussion

B. Have you encountered a demonic angel in your dreams?

Discussion

C. Why are people afraid of angels? Are you?

Discussion

Interactive Dreams and Visions

POINT TO NOTE

1. The seer is also more likely to have frequent *interactive* dreams and visions than most other prophets. In an interactive dream there is an exchange between the dreamer and God during the spiritual encounter. For appropriate interaction with God in dreams and visions, there needs to be a certain level of natural consciousness; for instance, knowing who you are and what you would normally stand for in your natural life during the dream encounter. King Abimelek had this required degree of retained consciousness in this encounter:

   > *Now Abraham moved on from there into the region of the Negev and lived between Kadesh and Shur. For a while he stayed in Gerar, and there Abraham said of his wife Sarah, "She is my sister." Then Abimelek king of Gerar sent for Sarah and took her.* ***But God came to Abimelek in a dream*** *one night and said to him,* ***"You are as good as dead because of the woman you have taken; she is a married woman."*** *Now Abimelek had not gone near her, so he said,* ***"Lord, will you destroy an innocent nation? Did he not say to me, 'She is my sister,' and didn't she also say, 'He is my brother'? I have done this with a clear conscience and clean hands."*** *Then God said to him the dream,* ***"Yes, I know you did this with a clear conscience, and so I have kept you from sinning against me. That is why I did not let you touch her.*** *Now return the man's wife, for he is a prophet, and he will pray for you and you will live. But if you do not return her, you may be sure that you and all yours will die"* (Genesis 20:1-7).

   As did Apostle Peter in the visionary encounter recorded in Acts 10:9-20.

EXERCISES

A. Do you have a spiritual encounter with God during your dreams?

   Discussion

   ___

   ___

   ___

B. Do you retain a level of adequate natural consciousness while dreaming?

   Discussion

   ___

   ___

   ___

C. Have you had a similar experience as Peter (see Acts 10:9-20)?

Discussion

Ministry Seasons

POINTS TO NOTE

1. During seasons of low revelatory receptivity it is best to develop dependency on the supremacy of God. The prophet Ezekiel experienced many seasons of highs and lows. One of God's seasons was an incredible period of divinely instituted silence (see Ezek. 33:21-22). Ezekiel experienced silence for about seven years until an exile arrived in Babylon with the news of the fall of Jerusalem. God ended Ezekiel's long silence just before the man got to him, by which time Ezekiel had learned valuable lessons. After the arrival of the exile to Babylon, the tone of Ezekiel's message changed from that of doom to prophecies of hope for the broken people of Judah. Seasons of low revelatory receptivity or divine silence can be a time to imbibe a paradigm shift from God (see Ezek. 33:23-34).
2. There are also seasons when revelations may be plentiful. The seer must be conscious of the fact that it is God who gives revelations, that prerogatives will forever remain His, and those who dwell in the secret place of the Most High shall abide under the shadow of the Almighty (see 2 Peter 1:20-23AMP).
3. In the days of the prophet Jeremiah, some desperate people compelled the prophets to interpret their dreams whether they had received any meaning or not. To save face, prophets made up stories. This is obviously dangerous—unless God gives the revelation, the prophet receives nothing. In a way, the prophetic person is like a postman and should not feel badly if the mail is scarce.

EXERCISES

A. Have you experienced seasons of low revelatory receptivity?

Discussion

B. Seasons of low revelatory receptivity or divine silence could be a time to absorb a paradigm shift from God.

Discussion

C. Have you ever or have you heard someone give a revelation that wasn't true, just to appease others?

Discussion

Value Uniqueness and Allow No Sentimentality

POINTS TO NOTE

1. ***Prophetic Uniqueness***

   Amos was a farmer when he was called into ministry and a prophet for the most part; he used a plain writing style, filled with strong country language that reflected his farmer background (see Amos 1:1).

   > *Hear this word,* ***you cows*** *[meaning people] of Bashan on Mount Samaria, you women who oppress the poor and crush the needy and say to your husbands, "Bring us some drinks!"* (Amos 4:1)

2. ***Avoid Sentiment***

   Sentimentality has no place in a seer or prophet's ministry. Sentiment is an emotion and comes from your soul part. God had to warn the prophet Ezekiel when he was overwhelmed by what he saw in the natural. As a result, he sat unable to express or deliver his message for seven days until he received God's warning (see Ezek. 3:14-19). The seer or prophet should move only in the compassion and mercies of God and not in emotions that natural circumstances dictate.

EXERCISES

A. Are you sometimes overwhelmed by what you see in the natural?

Discussion

B. Has God ever had to warn you as He did Ezekiel?

Discussion

C. Do you move only in the compassion and mercies of God and not in emotions that natural circumstances dictate?

Discussion

PRACTICAL PRINCIPLES AND DISCUSSION

CHAPTER 25

The Body's Lamp

RTM

The Eye Gate—Lamp of the Body

POINTS TO NOTE

1. The eye gate is the sensory gate by which you perceive or receive visual revelation of information. *The eye gate functionally consists of the natural eyes, the spiritual eyes, how the two work, and how the human eyes influence the light within you.* The eye gate is an important door into humans.

2. The Bible says that the eyes are the "lamp of the body." A good eye is symbolized as a useful lamp and it gives true enlightenment to the whole body:

   > ***Your eye is the lamp of your body.*** *When your eyes are healthy, your whole body also is full of light. But when they are unhealthy, your body also is full of darkness. See to it, then, that the light within you is not darkness. Therefore, if your whole body is full of light, and no part of it dark, it will be just as full of light as when a lamp shines its light on you* (Luke 11:34-36).

   Proper functioning of the eye gate is crucial for the effectiveness of seeing in the spirit realm. Evidence abounds to the significant role and the addictive nature of the eye gate in capturing the human attention. The human mind processes thoughts, ideas, and concepts in pictures, which have a gripping effect on the imagination, and the pictures are often hard to erase. Impressions logged into your imagination are long lasting—be careful what you let in through your eye gate.

3. Many people have rightly called the prophetic ministry the eye of the Body of Christ. Indeed this is why the prophet Isaiah described the darkness associated with the disobedience to God as prophetic blindness:

   > *Be stunned and amazed, blind yourselves and be sightless; be drunk, but not from wine, stagger, but not from beer. The Lord has brought over you a deep sleep: He has sealed your eyes (the prophets); He has covered your heads (the seers). For you this whole vision is nothing but words sealed in a scroll. And if you give the scroll to someone who can read, and say to him, "Read this, please," he will answer, "I can't; it is sealed." Or if you give the scroll to someone who cannot read, and say, "Read this, please," he will answer, "I don't know how to read." The Lord says: "These people come near to me with their mouth and honor Me with their lips, but their hearts are far from Me. Their worship of Me is made up only of rules taught by men. Therefore once more I will astound these people with wonder upon wonder; the wisdom of the wise will perish, the intelligence of the intelligent will vanish"* (Isaiah 29:9-14).

EXERCISES

A. How do you describe the "light within you"?

Discussion

B. Are you very careful about what you let in through your eye gate? What precautions do you take on a routine basis?

Discussion

C. Considering Isaiah 29:9-14, do you agree that the prophetic ministry could be accurately called the eye of the Body of Christ?

Discussion

Seeing into the Spirit Realm

POINTS TO NOTE

1. The main essence of the ministry of the watchman is to see into the spirit realm and report to the people. If a watchman is blind, he or she has virtually lost the core of the ministry:

> *Come, all you beasts of the field, come and devour, all you beasts of the forest! Israel's watchmen are blind, they all lack knowledge...* (Isaiah 56:9-19).

2. Never forget that satan is after the human eye gate to pollute, hijack, or corrupt its functionality (see Gen. 3:4-5). The eye gate was probably the first perceptive sense to be affected when man fell into sin in the Garden of Eden:

   > *When the woman saw that the fruit of the tree was good for food and pleasing to the eye, and also desirable for gaining wisdom, she took some and ate it. She also gave some to her husband, who was with her, and he ate it.* ***Then the eyes of both of them were opened****, and they realized that they were naked; so they sewed fig leaves together and made coverings for themselves* (Genesis 3:6-7).

3. Once the natural eyes were opened and activated, human reasoning was triggered into action, and has continued to grow exponentially. Unfortunately, there has been a corresponding dampening of humankind's ability to see into the spirit realm. However, the plan and purpose of God concerning your spiritual visual acuity will continue to be:

   > *...that the God of our Lord Jesus Christ, the glorious Father, may give you the Spirit of wisdom and revelation, so that you may know him better. ...that the eyes of your heart may be enlightened in order that you may know the hope to which he has called you, the riches of his glorious inheritance in the saints, and his incomparably great power for us who believe...* (Ephesians 1:17-19).

EXERCISES

A. What are some ways that a watchman is blinded, which results in the loss of the core of the ministry?

Discussion

____

____

____

B. Why do you think that the first perceptive sense to be affected by the Fall was the eye gate?

Discussion

____

____

____

C. Do you agree with Paul that your eyes will be enlightened?

Discussion

____

____

____

The Power of the Eye Gate

POINTS TO NOTE

1. The eye gate *is connected to your memory and intellect, influences your soul, and arouses emotions.* When emotions are high, your will often succumbs and your mind is inevitably dragged along. When this happens, *reasoning, caution, and etiquette* are discarded. As a consequence, *righteousness takes a pathetic second place*.
2. The power of the eye gate was demonstrated in the beginning of human existence. With his unpolluted and unadulterated eye gate, Adam could see, observe, and name the animals (see Gen. 2:19-20). In this instance, humankind using the pure state of the eye gate, scored 100 percent from God's viewpoint.
3. Because your eyes can receive from the natural *and* the spiritual realms, you should be very mindful about what you allow in spiritually *and* naturally. Most often you become what you behold. Job said; *"I made a covenant with my eyes not to look lustfully at a young woman"* (Job 31:1). David said, *"I will not look with approval on anything that is vile. I hate what faithless people do; I will have no part in it"* (Ps. 101:3). Ultimately, *you* can let in light or darkness. *If you give your eyes to the Lord for His kingdom purposes, you become the light of the world.*

EXERCISES

A. Names some ways that your eye gate influences your soul.

Discussion

___

___

___

B. Have you made a covenant, like Job, with your eyes? Should you?

Discussion

___

___

___

C. Have you determined to set before your eyes no vile thing?

Discussion

___

___

___

Spiritual Eyes

POINTS TO NOTE

1. Spiritual eyes are the eye of faith and the eye of the heart or understanding, and the eye sense by which you navigate the spirit realm. *Unlike your natural eyes, spiritual eyes have multidimensional functionalities and can see into the natural and spiritual realms without the limitation of time, space, and height.* This is the eye sense by which prophecy, dreams, and most visions are received. Symbolically this is the eye sense through which illumination or divine understanding comes in to clarify an issue. The spiritual eye is figuratively also the eye of hope. For some, most of the revelations that they receive are through spiritual eyes.
2. The Bible records that Moses used his spiritual eyes to look into the future and saw the One who is invisible to the natural eyes:

   > ***By faith*** *he left Egypt, not fearing the king's anger; he persevered because* ***he saw him who is invisible*** (Hebrews 11:27).

3. The functionality of spiritual eyes is connected to the purity of the heart, being the eye of the heart, and determines whether or not you are able to see God. As the Scriptures say: *Blessed are the* ***pure in heart,*** *for they will* ***see God*** (Matt. 5:8). I can also call spiritual eyes the eye of understanding because the Bible says:

   > *Anyone who claims to be in the light but hates a brother or sister is still in the darkness. Anyone who loves their brother and sister lives in the light, and there is nothing in them to make them stumble. But anyone who hates a brother or sister is in the darkness and walks around in the darkness. They do not know where they are going, because the darkness has blinded them* (1 John 2:9-11; see also 2 Cor. 3:14; 4:4).

EXERCISES

A. If spiritual eyes are the eye of the heart or understanding, and the eye sense by which you navigate the spirit realm, are you on course to reach your God-given destiny?

Discussion

____

____

B. If the functionality of spiritual eyes is connected to the purity of the heart, are you able to see God?

Discussion

____

____

C. Do your spiritual eyes see 20/20?

Discussion

How the Eye Gate Components Work

POINTS TO NOTE

1. The components of the eye gate can work together:

   And the end of the time I, Nebuchadnezzar, ***lifted my eyes*** *to* ***heaven****, and my* ***understanding returned*** *to me...* (Daniel 4:34 NKJV).

   Here Nebuchadnezzar lifted his eyes (*natural eyes*) symbolically to Heaven (the spirit realm only via *the spiritual eyes*) and his understanding (*the light within him*) returned to him.

2. In many biblical instances, we are reminded that humankind is responsible for how the eye gate is used. It is therefore, a matter of determination to keep your eye gate pure.

   Turn my eyes away from worthless things; preserve my life according to your word (Psalm 119:37).

   I lift up my eyes to you, to you whose throne in heaven (Psalm 123:1).

   At the end of that time, I, Nebuchadnezzar, raised my eyes toward heaven, and my sanity was restored. Then I praised the Most High; I honored and glorified him who lives forever. His dominion is an eternal dominion; his kingdom endures from generation to generation (Daniel 4:34).

   Looking onto Jesus, the author and finisher of our faith... (Hebrews 12:2 NKJV).

EXERCISES

A. What are the three ways that the eye gate components work together?

Discussion

B. What are your responsibilities regarding your eye gate?

Discussion

C. On whom should your eyes always be fixed?

Discussion

PRACTICAL PRINCIPLES AND DISCUSSION

CHAPTER 26

The Watchman's Ministry and the Seer's Dimension

POINTS TO NOTE

1. The watchman ministry operates mostly from the seer's dimension of the prophetic ministry—there are *nabi* watchmen, even though I believe there is a substantial slant to receiving by visual revelations in most watchman ministries.
2. A key distinguishing feature of the watchman is that a great percent of dreams and other revelations *speak of nonpersonal issues*. Whereas for other dreamers, over 90 percent of received dreams or picture revelations *are personal*. This distinction is crucial for proper integration of this valuable gifting in the Body of Christ.
3. When watchmen's revelations are ignored, it leads to loss of valuable resources and unnecessary casualties in spiritual warfare. The true spiritual watchman must always be steadfast, always abiding on the side of God and withstanding hostility and religious dogmatism (see Hosea 9:8).
4. Watchmen are often timekeepers (see Isa. 21:11-12). The sons of Issachar were watchmen who had a special understanding of the signs of the times and seasons: *"Men of Issachar, who understood the times and knew what Israel should do—200 chiefs, with all their relatives under their command"* (1 Chron. 12:32).
5. Watchmen are also gatekeepers or often work closely with other gatekeepers, as illustrated by King David, the watchman and the gatekeeper in the story recorded in Second Samuel 18:24-27. Even in the New Testament, Jesus spoke about the watchman (see John 10:1-3). Thus the gate is closed if the watchman sees and reports in-coming evil or a dangerous approach. And the gate is then opened at the command of the king by advice based on what the watchman observes.

EXERCISES

A. Are you different from other dreamers, in that a great percent of your dreams and other revelations speak of nonpersonal issues?

Discussion

B. Are you steadfast, always abiding on the side of God, withstanding hostility and religious dogmatism of the people?

Discussion

C. Are you a gatekeeper who often works closely with other gatekeepers?

Discussion

Divinely Inspired Mandate

POINTS TO NOTE

1. Many times prophetic words from a watchman are full of woes, lament, or sadness. *Despite the fact that woes, laments, and sadness are common in most watchman's reports, the watchman ministry has the potential to bring strategic revelations and insightful knowledge of the exact time, name, and place of operation of specific evil forces or principalities that come against the people of God.*

2. For the most part, the watchman has a divinely inspired mandate to warn, which sometimes translates into insatiable urges to give frequent warnings in order for prayers to be offered and calamities averted. Sometimes there are near-compulsive urges to warn. This is why the prophet Micah said, *"Because of this I will weep and wail; I will go about barefoot and naked. I will howl like a jackal and moan like an owl"* (Micah 1:8).

   And Jeremiah also said:

   > *Whenever I speak, I cry out proclaiming violence and destruction. So the work of the Lord has brought me insult and reproach all day long. But if I say, "I will not mention his word or speak anymore in his name," his word is in my heart like a fire, a fire shut up in my bones. I am weary of holding it in; indeed, I cannot* (Jeremiah 20:8-9).

EXERCISES

A. How do you feel about delivering reports full of woes, lament, or sadness?

Discussion

B. Are you an effective watchman? Why or why not?

Discussion

C. Do you sometimes experience insatiable urges to give warnings so calamities can be averted?

Discussion

Intercession

POINTS TO NOTE

1. Watchmen may not function as effective intercessors, and not all intercessors have a watchman's anointing. *Nevertheless, intercession should be an integral part of the watchman's ministry.* The watchman measures success or effectiveness by not allowing most of his or her warning prophecies to come to pass. *The ultimate goal is that the warning is heeded and judgment averted.* Every watchman should strive to become an effective intercessor (see Ezek. 3:17).

2. Every watchman is appointed and called by God, and the call of the watchman should come with specifics of the roles and responsibilities of the job. The watchman is called to receive revelations from God and to deliver them to the people. *The call of the watchman is typified by the call of Ezekiel.* All watchmen should be called by and empowered by the Spirit of God. In the case of Ezekiel, the Spirit of God came upon and imparted to him divine enablement needed for his ministry (see Ezek. 2:2-8)

EXERCISES

A. Are you an effective intercessor?

Discussion

B. Write your insights after reading Ezekiel 2:2-8.

Discussion

C. Do you feel called and empowered by the Spirit of God?

Discussion

The Call

POINTS TO NOTE

1. Remember these important aspects of the watchman's call:

- The call contains the essence of the watchman's assignment as in Ezekiel 2.
- God's boldness and confidence for the assignment comes with the call.
- God equips and assures divine protection.
- God clarifies His desire and the need to speak the true message with boldness.
- The call also makes it clear that obedience to God is a prerequisite, so God warned Ezekiel not to be dissuaded by the circumstances.

- The watchman must not rebel against the local authority as illustrated by King David, the watchman, and the gatekeeper in the story told in Second Samuel 18:24-27.

2. In Ezekiel's call, God emphasized the need to be grounded in the Word: *"Then I looked, and I saw a hand stretched out to me. In it was a scroll"* (Ezek. 2:9; see also Ezek. 3:1-3). Even at the beginning, in this case of Ezekiel, God hints that there would be propensity to the message of lament, mourning, or woes in the watchman's ministry and assignment: *"which he unrolled before me. On both sides of it were written words of lament and mourning and woe"* (Ezek. 2:10). *However, this should be handled with maturity to ensure acceptance of the watchman messages.*
3. God's call to Ezekiel also emphasized the need to understand the mission, and allow God to order each step of the way.

> *And He said to me, "Son of man, listen carefully and take to heart all the words I speak to you. Go now to your people in exile and speak to them. Say to them, 'This is what the Sovereign Lord says,' whether they listen or fail to listen"* (Ezekiel 3:10-11).

EXERCISES

A. Which aspect of the call is easiest for you to accept—the hardest?

Discussion

B. Are you prepared to handle your ministry with maturity to ensure acceptance of your messages?

Discussion

C. Do you understand the mission and allow God to order each step of the way?

Discussion

PRACTICAL PRINCIPLES AND DISCUSSION

CHAPTER 27

Preparing for Your Watchman's Ministry

POINTS TO NOTE

The following fundamentals provide insight into how you can prepare for a watchman's ministry:

1. ***The Watchman and the Word of God***

2. Prophets Ezekiel and Jeremiah and the apostle John had to *eat* the Word of God. See Ezekiel 3:1-3, Jeremiah 15:16, and Revelation 10:9-11. Also, the prophet Samuel had to learn the value of the Word of God early in his life (see 1 Sam. 3:7,19-21; 4:1).

3. ***Be Strong Physically and Emotionally***

   Isaiah experienced actual physical pains after he received the revelation; physical fitness is paramount to the watchman ministry (see Isa. 21:2-4).

4. ***Spiritual Alertness***

   An alert spirit is crucial for any effective watchfulness (see Isa. 21:1,5-6).

5. ***Strengthen the Spirit***

   To strengthen your spirit means to do what is necessary to bring your spirit into a right relationship with God and into a position of effectiveness—a place of minimal interference from the body and soul. This is also the place to maximize your capacity to receive and handle revelations from God: *"He who has no rule over his own spirit is like city that is broken down and without walls"* (Prov. 25:28 AMP).

6. ***A Solid Foundation***

   The watchman is stationed on an elevated wall and if the wall is broken down, the watchman loses that advantage (see Ps. 11:3; Lam. 2:9).

   A solid foundation includes other essential groups co-working with the watchman: intercessors; gatekeepers; local church leadership (and the local church); good, stable family life; other watchers.

7. ***Right Standing with God***

   The psalmist tells us that if God is not watching over a city, the watchmen labor in vain (see Ps. 127:1). Also, the prophet Hosea said, *"The prophet, along with my God, is the watchman over Ephraim"* (Hosea 9:8a). The watchman needs to rely on God. The psalmist also says, the Lord confides in those who fear Him.

8. ***Recognize That Satan is a Counterfeit Watchman***

   The watchman needs to be aware of satan and conscious that the enemy and his agents are watching. Always remember that satan is a counterfeit watchman:

The wicked watches the righteous, and seeks to slay him (Psalm 37:32 NKJV).

Do not enter the path of the wicked. And do not walk in the way of evil. Avoid it, do not travel on it; turn away from it a pass on. For they do not sleep unless they have done evil, and their sleep is taken away unless they make someone fall (Proverbs 4:14-16 NKJV).

Be sober, be vigilant; because your adversary the devil walks about like a roaring lion, seeking whom he may devour (1 Peter 5:8 NKJV).

EXERCISES

A. Of the seven fundamental aspects of the watchman's ministry, would you rank them as stated, or would you rearrange the order of importance?

Discussion

B. What circumstance facilitates a watchman standing guard in vain over a city?

Discussion

C. Why is it important to be sober and vigilant?

Discussion

Four Basic Functions and Three Main Watches

POINTS TO NOTE

The Old Testament often serves as a type and symbol of things that happen in the spirit realm. In the Old Testament there were at least four basic functions and three main watches of four hours each for the watchman.

1. The Four Basic Functions

    - To watch out for the enemy without creating rancor and acrimony within the camp.
    - To watch for the king or other members of royal family (the coming of Jesus Christ or divine messenger), and to announce their coming to the city so that they might be received with the proper protocols. When the Ark of God was returned to the Israelites unexpectedly, seventy people were struck down because they did not receive it with the proper protocol (see 1 Sam. 6:13-15, 19-20). To encourage the righteous in his righteousness and to warn the wicked to turn from his wickedness (see Ezek. 33:12-14).
    - The prophetic watchman is also to tell of the times: *"Men of Issachar, who understood the times and knew what Israel should do—200 chiefs, with all their relatives under their command"* (1 Chron. 12:32).
    - The watchman anointing and prayer is the "watch and pray principle." A watchman needs to be prayerful because the elevated spiritual position not only creates a vantage point, but also exposes him or her to the radar of the enemy.

2. The Three Main Watches

    The watches were times of the night assigned for spiritual watchfulness or alertness. There are two systems of nomenclature in Bible days: 1) the "Jew's recording" and the "Old Testament writings" named the watches differently from the Roman's recording, and 2) the "New Testament writing." The Jews divided the night into three parts of four hours each and the Romans divided the night into four of three hours each (see Lam. 2:19). As watchmen in the natural world could not watch 24 hours every day, the spiritual watchmen should likewise collaborate with each other in other ministry to avoid fatigue.

    The first watch is the evening watch (see Lam. 2:19) and is for apostolic specifications of the mandate to the watchman. It is the watch for impartation, consolidation, and motivation of the specifics of the mission to the watchman.

    The middle watch is mentioned in Judges 7:19 and is:

    - The time of most vulnerability because this is when most people are asleep.
    - A time the devil uses to sow weeds among the wheat (see Matt.13:25).
    - A time for intensive spiritual activities—prayers and consecration.
    - The midnight hour when the angel of death passed through Egypt.
    - A time the soul and body are least active, therefore a time of enhanced spiritual receptivity and vulnerability.

- When the angel of the Lord released Paul and Silas.
- A time when the spiritual atmosphere is susceptible to change.
- When Gideon destroyed the altars of Baal; therefore a time for spiritual warfare for the destruction of idolatry and other demonic practices.

The last watch is mentioned in First Samuel 11:11 and Exodus 14:23-25 and is a time:

- To watch and move in the confidence of what God has done in the previous watches.
- For stirring up people as empowered by the Spirit of God.
- To strategize using the privilege of the revelations received in the previous watches.
- To act out and move out in faith.
- To call for divine validation and intervention.

EXERCISES

A. How comfortable are you with encouraging the righteous in their righteousness and warning the wicked to turn from their wickedness?

Discussion

B. Why is the middle watch the time of most vulnerability?

Discussion

C. How did God use the last watch to benefit His people as told in Exodus 14:23-25?

Discussion

PRACTICAL PRINCIPLES AND DISCUSSION

CHAPTER 28

The Essence of a Watchman

The Attitude and Essence of a True Spiritual Watchman

POINTS TO NOTE

1. In Genesis 18:17-32, Abraham typified the correct attitude of an effective watchman:

    - A watchman should be continually ready. Abraham's spiritual alertness enabled him to see the unconventional arrival of the celestial beings.
    - A watchman should be spiritually sensitive enough to discern a move of God.
    - A watchman should live a life full of kindness. Abraham was prepared to entertain strangers (see Heb. 13:2).
    - A watchman's strength lies in his intimacy with God. God describes Abraham as a friend. Intimacy with God determines what a watchman receives and places the watchman in a position to intercede for others. *This is the privilege that allowed Abraham to question God.*
    - A watchman should be a friend of God.

2. *A watchman with "volumes of revelations" but who lacks the essence of the will and purpose of God will send confused signals.* We need watchmen such as Daniel, who discovered Jeremiah's prophecy and prayed it through (see Dan. 9:1-3). The watchman should ensure that prophecy and progress should go together (see Isa. 62:6-7).

3. Jesus Christ Himself is a true spiritual watchman. He said, *"Very truly I tell you, the Son can do nothing by himself; he can do only what he sees his Father doing, because whatever the Father does the Son also does"* (John 5:19). Jesus also taught His disciples to pray, *"Your kingdom come, your will be done on earth as it is in heaven"* (Matt. 6:10). *Unless it exists in Heaven, it cannot be brought into the reality of an earthly existence.* So the true essence of the spiritual watchman is to give warnings and other revelations that align the earth to the plans and purposes of God.

4. Bring Good News! The role of the watchman is also to announce the good news of restoration to God (see Isa. 52:7-8). These good news announcements are missing in most existing watchman ministries today because they have *restricted themselves to operate only in the "warn them" dimension.* The watchman ministry should also prepare people to receive the coming of the King with proper protocol.

EXERCISES

A. Abraham had the correct attitude—what makes him such a good example?

Discussion

B. Are you a good example of a watchman with the correct attitude?

Discussion

C. Are good news announcements missing from the watchman ministries you are aware of?

Discussion

Essential Watchman Attributes—Submission and Cooperation

POINTS TO NOTE

1. Submission to authority, accountability, and cooperation with leadership as well as other ministries increases the credibility of the watchman. Credibility is earned—*no matter how anointed you are, you need to gain reasonable credibility for your messages to be accepted.*
2. A watchman must work in unity with other ministries—those with the gift of interpretation and those with the gift of application. The application of revelation should really come from the pastoral level and the interpretations from those who are gifted in interpretation and/or have a Daniel 1:17 anointing. *Corporately—the watchman, the pastor, and the gifted interpreter—should work together* (see 2 Sam. 18:24-27).

Watchmen are also linked and work closely with gatekeepers; the gate is closed if the watchman sees and reports evil or danger. When this level of cooperation is missing, your efforts become ineffective, irrelevant, and allow the enemy to sneak through the loopholes.

The basic role of the watchman is simply to watch and report to the people, even though some watchmen may sometimes lack the understanding of what he or she receives.

3. The fundamental and ultimate purpose of the watchman ministry is to align the people to the purposes of God, expose the plans of the enemy, and to bring God's purposes to the domain:

> *"I looked for someone among them who would build up the wall and stand before me in the gap on behalf of the land so I would not have to destroy it, but I found no one. So I will pour out my wrath on them and consume them with my fiery anger, bringing down on their own heads all they have done, declares the Sovereign Lord"* (Ezekiel 22:30-31).

It is vital to remember that God is the Supreme Watchman:

> *He will not let your foot slip—**he who watches** over you will not slumber; indeed, he who watches over Israel will neither slumber nor sleep. The **Lord watches** over you—the Lord is your shade at your right hand; the sun will not harm you by day, nor the moon by night. The Lord will keep you from all harm—**he will watch** over your life; **the Lord will watch** over your coming and going both now and forevermore* (Psalm 121:3-8).

4. Divine communication with each watchman is unique as it differs in the way they receive and express their gifting. Watchmen have different personalities, backgrounds, and methods for receiving and presenting revelations; some may be predominantly seers (Apostle John) and others *nabi* prophets (Isaiah).

EXERCISES

A. Are you increasing your credibility by submitting to authority, accountability, and cooperating with leadership as well as other ministries?

Discussion

B. Are your efforts ineffective and irrelevant because you are not being cooperative?

Discussion

C. What type of language do you use to convey your messages?

Discussion

Spiritual Reconnaissance and Surveillance

POINTS TO NOTE

1. The Bible emphasizes the critical roles and values of spiritual surveillance, reconnaissance, and discernment in effective spiritual warfare. Much has been written about the place of spiritual mapping as a vital strategy, but it remains only part of the whole story. *Spiritual mapping is the process of correctly identifying the nature, strength, history, methods of operation, and the legality of the enemy forces in an area.* But even as we do this, the enemy is also keeping a watchful eye on us. For a complete and correct perspective, watchmen need to know their roles in spiritual reconnaissance, surveillance, and discernment with equal fervency when watching for the approaching enemy.
2. *Spiritual surveillance is keeping watch over an opposing force (gives us how to prepare and protect the domain)*; you should keep watch over the enemy forces. The majority of unnecessary casualties in spiritual warfare is due to the saints of God failing to acknowledge the spiritual surveillance of evil forces. Satan has a formidable network of information gathering (see Job 1:7 NKJV).
3. Jesus Christ admonished us to be alert—that demons walk about looking and watching for places to rest, *"When an unclean spirit goes out of a person, it goes through arid places, seeking rest"* (Matt. 12:43a). And speaking to the same subject, Peter said, *"Be sober, be vigilant; because your adversary the devil walks about like a roaring lion, seeking whom he may devour"* (1 Pet. 5:8 NKJV).
4. Always be mindful that the devil's surveillance is formidable, coherent, and can be persistent. This is why the Bible says to give the devil no foothold. Watchmen need to keep ahead of the enemy and alert the people of the enemy's surveillance so they can minimize the loopholes in their midst. Also take courage in the fact that the Lord watches over the righteous ones; He who watches over Israel neither sleeps nor slumbers. Keep your mind steadfast on Him, as the Bible teaches, *"For the eyes of the Lord range throughout the earth to strengthen those whose hearts are fully committed to him..."* (2 Chron. 16:9).
5. *Spiritual reconnaissance surveys the enemy forces for military purposes (teaches us how to attack the enemy).* This includes spiritual mapping. Do this to be effective in spiritual warfare, as seen in the story of Moses and the Israelites when God allowed Moses to send men to spy out the Promised Land: *"The Lord said to Moses, 'Send*

some men to explore the land of Canaan, which I am giving to the Israelites. From each ancestral tribe send one of its leaders'" (Num. 13:1-2).

And again Joshua used this strategy:

> *Then Joshua son of Nun secretly sent two spies from Shittim. "Go, look over the land," he said, "especially Jericho." So they went and entered the house of a prostitute named Rahab and stayed there* (Joshua 2:1).

> *Then the two men started back. They went down out of the hills, forded the river and came to Joshua son of Nun and told him everything that had happened to them. They said to Joshua, "The Lord has surely given the whole land into our hands; all the people are melting in fear because of us"* (Joshua 2:23-24).

6. Spiritual reconnaissance (plans for attack) without proper spiritual surveillance (watch over enemy's plans) backup is dangerous and makes the domain vulnerable.
7. Good spiritual reconnaissance should be followed by appropriate response to the findings. When Israel conducted adequate spiritual reconnaissance but failed to discern that God was unhappy with them because of Achan's sin, they suffered defeat by a much smaller force in Ai (see Josh. 7:2-6).
8. Watchmen need to alert people of the enemy's reconnaissance. The city of Laish lacked effective spiritual watchmen and failed to recognize Israel's reconnaissance. This story illustrates the fate that could befall a quiet and peaceful city of a people who pay no attention to the danger of the enemy's spiritual mapping. The people of Laish were very unsuspecting so they became easy prey to their enemy:

> *So the five men left and came to Laish, where they saw that the people were living in safety, like the Sidonians,* [unsuspecting] *at peace and secure. And since their land lacked nothing, they were prosperous. Also, they lived a long way from the Sidonians and had no relationship with anyone else* (Judges 18:7).

It is important to remember that these Old Testament stories are types and symbols of the things of the supernatural. The enemy did a good job in spiritual mapping Samson's source of power. The Philistines knew they had to discover the secret behind Samson's supernatural power if they were to overcome him:

> *Some time later, he fell in love with a woman in the Valley of Sorek whose name was Delilah. The rulers of the Philistines went to her and said, "See if you can lure him into showing you the secret of his great strength and how we can overpower him so that we may tie him up and subdue him. Each one of us will give you eleven hundred shekels of silver"* (Judges 16:4-5).

EXERCISES

A. Define spiritual reconnaissance.

Discussion

B. Define spiritual surveillance.

Discussion

C. Do you have a modern-day story that illustrates the fate of a city of a people who pay no attention to the danger of the enemy's spiritual mapping?

Discussion

CHAPTER 29

The Importance of Discernment

POINTS TO NOTE

1. Spiritual discernment *is to perceive clearly something that lies beneath the surface*—the real motive or force behind the scene of an outward manifestation. Like faith, there is discernment as a gift of the Holy Spirit and there is discernment that every Christian should attain and nurture in the their lives. Discernment should be distinguished from the outworking of the suspicion of the mind.

   Discernment is a supernatural ability to know the source, nature, and activities of the Spirit (or spirits) at work in a situation. Discernment helps you know which spirit is at work, whether the Holy Spirit, human spirit, or the spirit of the devil and his agents.

2. You can discern what spirit is in operation by spiritual senses. For instance, you can discern by sight, hearing, smelling, or even by the sense of touch. The spiritual principle inherent in Hebrews 5:14 is valuable: *"But solid food is for the mature, who by constant use have trained themselves to distinguish good from evil."* The key words are *solid food* or (strong meat), which means in-depth understanding of deep things. Maturity comes with exercising your senses to discern good or evil.

   Key factors:

   - Obedience to the Lord
   - Relying on the truth
   - Allowing the Lord's compassion to consume you
   - Allowing forgiveness to prevail rather than sentiment judged by the flesh

   Remembering these key factors allows you to avoid sentiment. God's compassion is greater than any depth of human sentiment, and no one can be more compassionate than God. The most common hindrance to discernment is when people allow sentiment to cloud the nudging of the Holy Spirit. The Gibeonites deceived Joshua and the Israelites because they based their decision on what their natural senses and sentiments of the time dictated. *They did not seek the Lord and had no watchmen who could see beyond the surface* (see Josh. 9:14-16).

   Many people have suffered severe consequences because they allowed their sentiments to compromise the gentle but clear nudging of God discerned by revelations. The truth that must be said is that God knows the end from the beginning, even when your natural inclination runs contrary to what you discerned.

   The value of discernment cannot be overemphasized in the ministry of the watchman. The prophet Isaiah immediately spotted King Hezekiah's lack of discernment when the envoy from Babylon visited him (see 2 Kings 20:12-18). The apostle Paul and Silas discerned the spirit at work in the slave girl even though what she said was true:

> *Once when we were going to the place of prayer, we were met by a female slave who had a spirit by which she predicted the future. She earned a great deal of money for her owners by fortune-telling. She followed Paul and the rest of us, shouting, "These men are servants of the Most High God, who are telling you the way to be saved." She kept this up for many days. Finally Paul became so annoyed that he turned around and said to the spirit, "In the name of Jesus Christ I command you to come out of her!" At that moment the spirit left her. When her owners realized that their hope of making money was gone, they seized Paul and Silas and dragged them into the marketplace to face the authorities* (Acts 16:16-19).

On a personal level, the patriarch Isaac failed to heed the quiet and gentle nudging from the Holy Spirit and acted contrary to his discernment:

> *He went to his father and said, "My father." "Yes, my son," he answered. "Who is it?" Jacob said to his father, "I am Esau your firstborn. I have done as you told me. Please sit up and eat some of my game, so that you may give me your blessing." Isaac asked his son,* ***"How did you find it so quickly, my son?"*** *"The Lord your God gave me success," he replied. Then Isaac said to Jacob, "Come near so I can touch you, my son, to know whether you really are my son Esau or not." Jacob went close to his father Isaac, who touched him and said,* ***"The voice is the voice of Jacob, but the hands are the hands of Esau."*** *He did not recognize him, for his hands were hairy like those of his brother Esau; so he proceeded to bless him. "Are you really my son Esau?" he asked. "I am," he replied. Then he said, "My son, bring me some of your game to eat, so that I may give you my blessing." Jacob brought it to him and he ate; and he brought some wine and he drank. Then his father Isaac said to him, "Come here, my son, and kiss me." So he went to him and kissed him.* ***When Isaac caught the smell of his clothes, he blessed him*** *and said, "Ah, the smell of my son is like the smell of a field that the Lord has blessed* (Genesis 27:18-27).

Notice the levels of Isaac's failure to heed the nudging of spiritual discernment:

- "How did you find it so quickly, my son? (as he was quickened to ask by the Holy Spirit).
- "The voice is the voice of Jacob, but the hands are the hands of Esau" (he was nudged by Holy Spirit).
- "When Isaac caught the smell of his clothes, he blesses him" (his judgment was clouded by his natural perception).
- Finally, notice he allowed the perception by natural senses to override his inner conviction.

Nehemiah, the one who rebuilt the walls of Jerusalem, was ridiculed and threatened by those who opposed the rebuilding. Later he came under a new tactic of the enemy—psychological warfare—intimidation and deception. On several occasions Nehemiah discerned the schemes of the enemy behind the scene:

> *When word came to Sanballat, Tobiah, Geshem the Arab and the rest of our enemies that I had rebuilt the wall and not a gap was left in it—though up to that time I had not set the doors in the gates—Sanballat and Geshem sent me this message: "Come, let us meet together in one of the*

> *villages on the plain of Ono." But they were scheming to harm me; so I sent messengers to them with this reply: "I am carrying on a great project and cannot go down. Why should the work stop while I leave it and go down to you?" Four times they sent me the same message, and each time I gave them the same answer* (Nehemiah 6:1-4).

In this instance, Nehemiah discerned that beneath the apparent good will suggestion given to him was a ploy to lure him into disobeying God; so he resisted the temptation.

> *One day I went to the house of Shemaiah son of Delaiah, the son of Mehetabel, who was shut in at his home [Shemaiah was said to be receiving messages from God] the son of Mehetabel. He said, "Let us meet in the house of God, inside the temple, and let us close the temple doors, because men are coming to kill you—by night they are coming to kill you." But I said,* ***"Should a man like me run away? Or should someone like me go into the temple to save his life? I will not go!"*** (Nehemiah 6:10-11)

EXERCISES

A. Were you aware that you can discern what spirit is in operation by using your spiritual and natural senses?

Discussion

B. Are you relying consistently on the four key factors to keep sentiment from clouding your spiritual discernment?

Discussion

C. Have you suffered consequences of allowing your sentiments to compromise adherence to the gentle but clear nudging of God discerned by revelations?

Discussion

Distinguishing Discernment from Judgment and a Suspicious Mind

POINTS TO NOTE

1. When a watchman discerns a danger or a point of vulnerability as a result of weakness, he or she warns the people with **an *admonishment.*** When admonishment is not ***cushioned by inspiration***, it is ***judgment***. Whenever a watchman warns or admonishes without giving hope to the people, *it is* ***condemnation. Admonishment*** plus ***hope*** is ***motivation***. Admonishment calls or warns people to move from a place weakness, vulnerability, or unrighteousness to a place of right standing with God. An immature watchman warns and then leaves the people in condemnation without hope. They often take the place of judge over the people, but the Bible says mercy triumphs over judgment (see James 2:13). *The cardinal purpose of the watchman's ministry is to avoid calamity.*

2. The critical issue for most people, including watchmen, is how to differentiate suspicion of their minds and judging by the flesh from the gentle nudging from the Holy Spirit, which is spiritual discernment. I use the following ways to distinguish the difference:

   - By living in the Word of God. The greatest discerner on earth is the Word of God:

     > *For the word of God is living and active. Sharper than any double-edged sword, it penetrates even to dividing soul and spirit, joints and marrow;* ***it judges*** [the discerner of] *the thoughts and attitudes of the heart* (Hebrews 4:12).

   - By renewing the mind.

     > *Do not conform any longer to the pattern of this world, but be transformed by the renewing of your mind. Then you will be able to test and approve what God's will is—**His good, pleasing and perfect will*** (Romans 12:2).

   - By focusing on the things in Heaven rather than on the things on earth.

     > *Set your minds on things above, not on earthly things. For you died, and your life is now hidden with Christ in God* (Colossians 3:2-3).

   - By being of like mind with Jesus Christ.

     > *Therefore if you have any encouragement from being united with Christ, if any comfort from his love, if any common sharing in the Spirit, if any tenderness and compassion, then make my joy complete by being like-minded, having the same love, being one in spirit and of one mind. Do nothing out of selfish ambition or vain conceit. Rather, in humility value others above yourselves, not looking to your own interests but each of you to the interests of the others. In your relationships with one another, have the same mindset as Christ Jesus* (Philippians 2:1-5).

   - By keeping a clear and undefiled conscience.

     > *A person who is pure of heart sees goodness and purity in everything; but a person whose own heart is evil and untrusting finds evil in everything, for his dirty mind and rebellious heart color all he sees and hears* (Titus 1:15 TLB).

- By the transforming hand of the Holy Spirit.

  At that time the Spirit of the Lord will come mightily upon you, and you will prophesy with them and you will feel and act like a different person. From that time on your decisions should be based on whatever seems best under the circumstances, for the Lord will guide you (1 Samuel 10:6-7 TLB).

3. Every revelation confers *some degree of responsibility on the one who receives it*. With such responsibilities comes the diminution in the grace of God that accrues from the state of being unaware and innocent about the subject. The onus is on you to make a godly response to the revelations you receive, or are discerned by the Spirit—if you do not, you may suffer the consequences of ignoring it.

EXERCISES

A. Are you guilty of warning people and then leaving them in condemnation and without hope?

Discussion

B. How easy it is for you to differentiate suspicion of your mind and judging by the flesh from the gentle nudging from the Holy Spirit?

Discussion

C. Are you prepared to assume the responsibility of receiving every revelation that the Lord gives to you? Will you give a godly response?

Discussion

PRACTICAL PRINCIPLES AND DISCUSSION

CHAPTER 30

Beware of Opposing Spirits

POINTS TO NOTE

1. Be aware of the spirits that can come against the watchman. But be comforted and assured—***greater is He who is in you*** than he that is in the world! To be aware of evil spirits is to be forewarned and forearmed. Accept the following information as a weapon to use against satan and his agents.

The Spirit of Stupor

The evil of this spirit is the compelling, irresistible urge for intermittent sleepiness when you should be awake and alert. This spirit is dangerous for all, but is an especially destructive enemy to the watchman anointing. It wastes great potentials or resources, whether it comes as a result of judgment from God or from the work of the enemy. *"As it is written: 'God gave them a* ***spirit of stupor,*** *eyes that could not see and ears that could not hear, to this very day'"* (Rom. 11:8). Read also Isaiah 29:9-12.

When this spirit is sent from God as judgment, it comes with other limitations that are manifested in a diversity of ways:

- Words sealed in a scroll—meaning the inability to interpret things from God
- Loss of grace
- Loss of favor
- Inability to get help or compassion from other people

Repentance and prayers will overcome this spirit.

A Perverse Spirit

A perverse spirit causes cloudiness in vision, a lack of understanding, and poor rendering of vision. For some watchmen, it is not the lack of revelations but poor understanding due to visual cloudiness. Poor understanding is the result of poor rendering of the messages to the people:

> *The Lord hath mingled a perverse spirit in the midst thereof...* (Isaiah 19:14 KJV).
>
> *The Lord has sent a spirit of foolishness on them so that their suggestions are wrong* (Isaiah 19:14 TLB).

> *And these also stagger from wine and reel from beer: Priests and prophets stagger from beer and are befuddled with wine; they reel from beer, they stagger when seeing visions, they stumble when rendering decisions* (Isaiah 28:7).

The following helps overcome this spirit:

- Spending quality time in the presence of God
- Repentance and prayers
- Consistent right standing with God

The Spirit of Non-Acceptance by the Leadership

This spirit causes leaders not to listen to the watchman. However, there are many reasons why the leadership may not listen to the watchman. To be listened to and accepted, the watchman needs credibility and should be accountable to the leadership.

> *When Jeremiah had finished telling the people all the words of the Lord their God—everything the Lord had sent him to tell them—Azariah son of Hoshaiah and Johanan son of Kareah and all the arrogant men said to Jeremiah, "You are lying! The Lord our God has not sent you to say, 'You must not go to Egypt to settle there.' But Baruch son of Neriah is inciting you against us to hand us over to the Babylonians, so they may kill us or carry us into exile to Babylon." So Johanan son of Kareah and all the army officers and all the people disobeyed the Lord's command to stay in the land of Judah. Instead, Johanan son of Kareah and all the army officers led away all the remnant of Judah who had come back to live in the land of Judah from all the nations where they had been scattered. They also led away all those whom Nebuzaradan commander of the imperial guard had left with Gedaliah son of Ahikam, the son of Shaphan—the men, the women, the children and the king's daughters. And they took Jeremiah the prophet and Baruch son of Neriah along with them. So they entered Egypt in disobedience to the Lord and went as far as Tahpanhes* (Jeremiah 43:1-7).

The following attitudes help you eliminate this problem:

- Repentance and prayers
- Improving credibility issues
- Collaborative work with the leadership

It is important that acceptance comes at the point of commission, when God grants you favor with others. At the time of call, watchmen have favor with God so that revelations are abundant, but usually they do not come with a commensurate degree of acceptance. Acceptance comes over time with a good degree of credibility. However, the spirit of non-acceptance described here is different from the non-acceptance inevitable in the training period.

Other Spirits

In the following passage the prophet Isaiah describes some spirits that can come against the watchman or you:

> *Come, all you beasts of the field, come and devour, all you beasts of the forest!* ***Israel's watchmen are blind,*** *they all lack knowledge; they are all mute dogs, they cannot bark; they lie around and dream, they love to sleep. They are* ***dogs with mighty appetites;*** *they never have enough. They are* ***shepherds who lack understanding;*** *they all turn to their own way, they seek their own gain* (Isaiah 56:9-11).

> *A call to the savage beasts: Come on the run. Come, devour, beast barbarians! For Israel's watchmen are blind, the whole lot of them. They have no idea what's going on. They're dogs without sense enough to bark, lazy dogs, dreaming in the sun—But hungry dogs, they do know how to eat, voracious dogs, with never enough. And these are Israel's shepherds! They know nothing, understand nothing. They all look after themselves, grabbing whatever's not nailed down. "Come," they say, "let's have a party. Let's go out and get drunk!" And tomorrow, more of the same: "Let's live it up!"* (Isaiah 56:9-12 The Message)

The Spirit of Spiritual Blindness

If a watchman is blind, he or she has lost the core of the ministry: *"Come, all you beasts of the field, come and devour, all you beasts of the forest! Israel's watchmen are blind, they all lack knowledge."* As a watchman, the prophet Isaiah looked into the future and saw where other ungodly nations (beasts) were stirred up to attack Israel. This became simple because the watchmen of Israel were blind, lacking spiritual insights to the plans of the enemy, leaving the nation unprotected. Watchmen can be distracted by worldly desires.

The Spirit of Covetousness

Covetousness is a dangerous ploy of the enemy to derail the plans and purposes of God in your life. Your ministry requires singleness of heart and mind to carry out your assignment. When you become entangled in the pursuit of worldly pleasures, the anointing is subverted, to say the least: *"They are dogs with mighty appetites; they never have enough."*

The Spirit of Self-Centeredness

The watchman's ministry is for the protection and preservation of the people. Therefore, if you become self-centered, that purpose is defeated. Unfortunately, some watchmen have allowed the devil to lure them into self-centeredness: *"They are shepherds who lack understanding; they all turn to their own way, each seeks his own gain."*

The Spirit of Dumbness

Your main purpose is to look ahead and warn the people of any approaching danger or inform them of the next move of God. If you lose the ability to warn, you have become useless. As the Bible says, *"they are all mute dogs, they cannot bark."*

Discerning Spirits against the Local Church

A watchman's role is not only to watch out for approaching danger or messenger, but also to discern "wolves among the sheep." Apostle Paul warned the Ephesians to guard against this:

> *Keep watch over yourselves and all the flock of which the Holy Spirit has made you overseers. Be shepherds of the church of God, which He bought with His own blood. I know that after I leave, savage wolves will come in among you and will not spare the flock. Even from your own number men will arise and distort the truth in order to draw away disciples after them. So* ***be on your guard!*** *Remember that for three years I never stopped warning each of you night and day with tears* (Acts 20:28-31).

You can significantly minimize and maybe even avert division, acrimony, and rancor in the Body of Christ if you spot the moves of the devil and his agents in the midst of God's people. As apostle Peter admonishes, *"But there were also false prophets among the people, just as there will be false teachers among you. They will secretly introduce destructive heresies, even denying the sovereign Lord who bought them—bringing swift destruction on themselves. Many will follow their depraved conduct and will bring the way of truth into disrepute"* (2 Pet. 2:1-2).

God Himself commended the church at Ephesus for their vigilance in discerning the false apostles among them: *"I know how many good things you are doing. I have watched your hard work and your patience. I know you don't tolerate sin among your members, and you have carefully examined the claims of those who say they are apostles but are not. You have found out how they lie"* (Rev. 2:2 TLB).

There are spirits that may arise within the congregation that you should be able to discern and stop from infiltrating the local structure. As in the days when Moses led the Israelites out of Egypt, every local congregation is a mixed multitude of people, *"a mixed multitude went up with them also"* (Exod. 12:38 NKJV). Later we see that *"the mixed multitude who were among them yielded to intense craving; so the children of Israel also wept again and said: 'Who will give us meat to eat?'"* (Num. 11:4 NKJV). In every multitude of people, there is diversity of human spirits. Therefore, the issue for a local church is not whether diversity of human spirits will arise, but that when they do, these spirits are discerned and properly managed to minimize or curb unwanted effects.

A Contentious Spirit

Contention is usually about control. Most problems in the church come down to—who is in charge? A contentious person can never lead, because he or she has most probably never learned to follow. A contentious spirit is like a malignant cell; it can destroy the person and hinder the growth of the church. A person with a contentious spirit can be the door through which satan comes to do his work.

> *For where you have envy and selfish ambition, there you find disorder and every evil practice* (James 3:16).

> *For lack of wood the fire goes out, and where there is no whisperer, contention ceases* (Proverbs 26:20 AMP).

The contentious spirit does not submit to authority. Apostle John had to deal with it, *"I wrote to the church, but Diotrephes, who loves to be first, will not welcome us"* (3 John 1:9). A contentious spirit and the spirit of witchcraft go together. Only love can defeat these spirits.

> *Above all, love each other deeply, because love covers over a multitude of sins* (1 Peter 4:8).

Every watchman can discern when this spirit of contention is in operation. It is helpful to know the psychology of a person with a contentious spirit. The contentious person believes that:

- When others are set in their ways, they are obstinate; but when he is, he is being "firm."
- When others don't like someone, they are stubborn; but when he does not, it is "good judgment."
- When others treat someone with care, they are bribing the person; but when he treats this way, he is being "thoughtful."
- When others take time to do something well, they are lazy or slow; but when he does this, he is "meticulous."
- When others find fault and find flaws, they are critical; but when he does, he is "perceptive."
- When others dress well, they are extravagant; when he does, he is "tasteful."
- When others say what they think, they are spiteful; when he does, he is being "honest."
- When others take risks, they are reckless; but when he does, he is "brave."

The way out of this dangerous spirit is found in Philippians 4:8:

> *Finally, brothers and sisters, whatever is true, whatever is noble, whatever is right, whatever is pure, whatever is lovely, whatever is admirable—if anything is excellent or praiseworthy—think about such things.*
>
> *...Since you are eager for the gifts of the Spirit, try to excel in those that build up the church* (1 Corinthians 14:12).

Spirits of Witchcraft

The spirit of witchcraft is any spirit, other than the Spirit of God, that manipulates or controls others. The spirit of witchcraft is a common spirit that comes against the local church—the spirit of control, manipulation, and intimidation. In the case of Absalom, this spirit manifested as *manipulation* and in the case of Jezebel as *control.* In the case of King Saul, it was disobedience or *rebellion*. Samuel said, *"For rebellion is as the sin of witchcraft..."* (1 Sam. 15:23 NKJV).

In the Western hemisphere, this spirit is predominantly *manipulation*. In Africa, this spirit manifests as *self-mutilations and destruction*. In Asian countries, it is the spirit of *craftiness, deception, and control.*

The Spirit of Absalom

The spirit of Absalom subverts by manipulation. This is a special form of witchcraft spirit that steals the hearts of people by deception and pretence. Absalom flatters and influences people by manipulating human greed and lust for his own personal advantage.

How can you deal with the spirit of Absalom? An Absalom spirit always looks for an Ahithophel; so you must counter the strategy of Ahithophel. An Ahithophel is a person gifted in wisdom and counsel, but is *bitter and revengeful*. A person with an Absalom spirit always looks for angry and dissatisfied people. Watch out for these people. Pray to God to overcome any conspiracy. God will turn the counsel of Ahithophel into foolishness.

The Spirit of Saul

The spirit of Saul is hatred that comes from envy or jealousy, often the result of *failure to acknowledge what God is doing in the lives of subordinates*. Some spiritual leaders are guilty of the spirit of Saul. This politicking spirit causes division in the church and has led many great men to becoming unfruitful, murderers, and consumed with hatred.

How can you deal with the spirit of Saul? Continue in the will of God, even if it means serving God at the risk of your life, like David did when he faced the ferocity of hatred from Saul. Do not fight back—the battle belongs to God. Wait for God's timing. Do not touch the anointed of God as David did not touch Saul. Do not rejoice in the fall of God's anointed no matter how mean he is. Seek the counsel of God.

The Spirit of Gehazi

The spirit of Gehazi is greed, covetousness, insubordination, and the spirit of self-centeredness. This spirit attacks people with a weak inner self. A person with a weak inner self may have a strong spirit but a soul that is not ruled by the Spirit of God. Gehazi's spirit was strong because of the prophet Elisha; however, he failed to control his emotions (soul), which produced a weak inner self. *A soul that is not controlled by the Spirit leads to perversion despite a strong spirit.* Gehazi ended up with leprosy instead of double portions of anointing.

> *"Go in peace," Elisha said. After Naaman had traveled some distance, Gehazi, the servant of Elisha the man of God, said to himself, "My master was too easy on Naaman, this Aramean, by not accepting from him what he brought. As surely as the Lord lives, I will run after him and get something from him"* (2 Kings 5:19-20).

The Spirit of Miriam

The spirit of Miriam is prejudice and separatism or racism in a church and the spirit of pride that makes young ministers rise up against the spiritual leader. Because of the subtlety and the damaging effects of this spirit, God fights this spirit Himself.

> *Miriam and Aaron began to talk against Moses because of his Cushite wife, for he had married a Cushite." Has the Lord spoken only through Moses?" they asked. "Hasn't he also spoken through us?" And the Lord heard this. (Now Moses was a very humble man, more humble than anyone else on the face of the earth)* (Numbers 12:1-3).

One way to deal with this spirit of pride, particularly in young ministers, is to teach them how to serve in various capacities within the church before elevating them to positions of leadership. Apostle Paul said about young converts in becoming overseers, *"He must not be a recent convert, or he may become conceited and fall under the same judgment as the devil!"* (1 Tim. 3:6).

The Spirit of Delilah

The spirit of Delilah is betrayal. This spirit destroys with the kiss of death. Delilah is full of flattery and betrays trust and friendship. Delilah sows the seeds of distrust and discord and is relentless. It is always motivated by self-gain. The spirit of Delilah thrives on sexual lust and targets the seer's anointing of the leadership with the goal of plucking out the eyes of the prophetic, like the spirit of Delilah did to Samson (see Judg. 16:4-6).

The Spirit of Jezebel

The spirit of Jezebel is a high level form of the spirit of witchcraft that controls by remote manipulation. It is also powered from the unseen ruling power in the kingdom of darkness realm. The spectrum of activities of this devious spirit ranges from mild cases when victims are unaware of being used, to deep-rooted evil in people who bask in this evil spirit's power. Predominantly, females are involved, but this spirit has no gender preference—the springboard is sexual exploitation. Jezebel targets spiritual leadership, especially prophetic and intercessory ministries.

The spirit is named after Queen Jezebel, wife of King Ahab and represents the character and nature of her demonic influence:

> *He not only considered it trivial to* ***commit the sins*** *of Jeroboam son of Nebat, but he also* ***married Jezebel*** *daughter of Ethbaal king of the Sidonians, and began to serve Baal and worship him* (1 Kings 16:31).
>
> *You are to destroy the house of Ahab your master, and* ***I will avenge*** *the blood of my servants the prophets and the blood of all the Lord's servants shed by Jezebel* (2 Kings 9:7).
>
> *Nevertheless, I have this against you: You tolerate that woman Jezebel, who calls herself a prophetess. By her teaching* ***she misleads*** *my servants into sexual immorality and the eating of food sacrificed to idols* (Revelation 2:20).

In present days, this spirit's destruction cuts across family morality, power plays at work, the entertainment industry, and spiritual leadership. This spirit uses deception, infiltration, manipulation, and sexual laxity to control its victims.

A two-pronged strategy is necessary to defeat this spirit. First for those who are being used, the way out is confession, humility, godly repentance, and submission to the appropriate authority. For leaders who have to confront this spirit, wisdom and discernment is absolutely necessary.

The Spirit of Korah

The spirit of Korah is rebellion by subversion; it hates the singular authority of the church. This spirit emanates from men of renown and influence and prevents people from responding to constituted authority by the influence of people upper society. This is often the result of hollow and deceptive theology and stems from delusions of grandeur.

> *Korah son of Izhar, the son of Kohath, the son of Levi, and certain Reubenites—Dathan and Abiram, sons of Eliab, and On son of Peleth—became insolent and rose up against Moses. With them*

> *were 250 Israelite men, well-known community leaders who had been appointed members of the council. They came as a group to oppose Moses and Aaron and said to them, "You have gone too far! The whole community is holy, every one of them, and the Lord is with them. Why then do you set yourselves above the Lord's assembly?"* (Numbers 16:1-3)

How can you deal with the spirit of Korah? The book of Numbers has the answer:

> *He warned the assembly, "Move back from the tents of these wicked men! Do not touch anything belonging to them, or you will be swept away because of all their sins." So they moved away from the tents of Korah, Dathan and Abiram had come out and were standing with their wives, children and little ones at the entrances of their tents. Then Moses said, "This is how you will know that the Lord has sent me to do all these things and that it was not my idea: If these men die a natural death and experience only what usually happens to men, then the Lord has not sent me. But if the Lord brings about something totally new, and the earth opens its mouth and swallows them, with everything that belongs to them, and they go down alive into the realm of the dead, then you will know that these men have treated the Lord with contempt." As soon as he finished saying all this, the ground under them split apart and the earth opened its mouth and swallowed them and their households, and all those associated with Korah, together with their possessions* (Numbers 16:26-32).

Bringing the effect of this spirit out into the open and discussing it will dispel it. Also, people must disassociate themselves from Korah, because it destroys others by association.

The Spirit of Sanballat and Tobiah: Spirit of Distraction

The spirit of Sanballat and Tobiah is distraction emanating from people of influence. This spirit is empowered by associating with people in high places and thrives on favoritism and corruption. It is based on deceptive association or marriage. Sanballat's family married into the family of the high priest: *"One of the sons of Joiada son of Eliashib the high priest* ***was son-in-law to Sanballat*** *the Horonite. And I drove him away from me"* (Neh. 13:28).

Tobiah also had connections in high places:

> *Also, in those days the nobles of Judah were sending many letters to Tobiah, and replies from Tobiah kept coming to them. For many in Judah were under oath to him, since he was son-in-law to Shekaniah son of Arah, and his son Jehohanan had married the daughter of Meshullam son of Berekiah. Moreover, they kept reporting to me his good deeds and then telling him what I said. And Tobiah sent letters to intimidate me* (Nehemiah 6:17-19).
>
> *Before this, Eliashib the priest had been put in charge of the storerooms of the house of our God. He was closely associated with Tobiah* (Nehemiah 13:4).
>
> *And came back to Jerusalem. Here I learned about the evil thing Eliashib had done in providing Tobiah a room in the courts of the house of God. I was greatly displeased and threw all Tobiah's household goods out of the room. I gave orders to purify the rooms, and then I put back into them the equipment of the house of God, with the grain offerings and the incense* (Nehemiah 13:7-9).

Like many churches today, Nehemiah faced a daunting task—the state of apostate and to reverse the trend of desolation. Successfully galvanizing the support of the Jews, and fending off ridicule within its camp, Nehemiah was faced with a new strategy of the enemy—distractions in the form of Sanballat and Tobiah who were influential local politicians. There was evidence that they were of Jewish ancestry, though they preferred the political status quo.

> *When Sanballat heard that we were rebuilding the wall, he became angry and was greatly incensed. He ridiculed the Jews and in the presence of associates and the army of Samaria he said, "What are those feeble Jews doing? Will they restore their wall? Will they offer sacrifices? Will they finish in a day? Can they bring the stone back to life from the heaps of rubble—burned as they are?" Tobiah the Ammonite, who was at his side, said, "What they are building—even a fox climbing up on it, would break down their wall of stones!"* (Nehemiah 4:1-3)

God Himself eliminates this spirit. You need to remain steadfast in righteousness, focusing on the things of God. Avoid being lured into the path of distraction.

EXERCISES

A. Of all the evil spirits discussed, which one are you most and least concerned about? Why?

Discussion

B. Do the ways to deal with these spirits seem sufficient? Can you add more?

Discussion

C. What steps will you take daily to keep from being lured into the path of destruction from these spirits?

Discussion

PRACTICAL PRINCIPLES AND DISCUSSION

CHAPTER 31

Integrating Your Ministry

POINTS TO NOTE

1. Watchmen are gifted to receive picture revelations consistently and frequently; therefore, you should be trained to handle your revelations to benefit yourself and the local church. Hopefully the local church and leadership will provide a friendly atmosphere for your training, growth, and mentoring.
2. The following guidelines are useful for watchmen and church leaders:

The seer/watchman needs to:

- Train your physical body and soul and enhance your spirit to receive from God; wisely minister to the Body of Christ.
- Seek a place of maximal reception of divine revelations.
- Discipline your physical body to withstand and sustain the rigors of seeing into the spirit realm.
- Transform or renew your mind, control your emotions, and yield your will to God.
- Be strong and discerning in the spirit to see things in the spirit realm.
- Live a life of love; God is love; love is the hallmark of your discipleship.
- Dwell in the peace of God; the level of peace enjoyed determines the level of experience you have in God.
- Be totally yielded to the will of God.
- Invest in God-given potentials.
- Spend times of intimacy with God, have a worshiping and prayerful life.
- Know that the place for the richness of the Word of God cannot be overemphasized.
- Avoid undue pressure, tension, and busyness.
- Ensure proper accountability to leadership and responsibility to the local church.
- Avoid the spirit of lawlessness at all cost.
- Avoid using your revelations to manipulate others.

The local church needs to:

- Provide secure mentoring support for those in training.

- Provide a forum for prophetic people to learn and develop.
- Meet regularly with those in training.
- Encourage those in training to take responsibility for the outworking of their gift.
- Assist those in training to plan their future moves.
- Create a safe environment that allows for mistakes to be corrected in a godly way.

Interactions:

- The seer/watchman receives from God and submits to leadership with humility.
- The seer/watchman should not police the progress or the implementation of the revelation.
- Both the seer/watchman and the leadership should prayerfully interact to ensure the essence of the revelation is not lost.
- The leadership should know that most seers or watchmen receive warnings with heavy burdens that often urge them to speak woe. This burden should be carefully managed from both sides, otherwise it can become pervasive, having the capability to drive the seer to a reclusive life if not properly harnessed and managed.
- Both should know that is often difficult to determine time applications unless in exceptional revelations they come with a clear time frame.
- Apostles and pastors have better time application than the prophet except when God gives the time frame clearly in the revelation. This is because the apostle or pastor can see many parts of the whole as they are in the position to bring together the many parts seen by many prophets. On the other hand, prophets see only in parts.
- For understanding to develop, on a regular basis the leadership should create a forum to meet with the seer and to resolve any unnecessary tension.
- The seer in training needs acceptance, and sometimes correction, to facilitate maturity in the anointing.
- Leaders should give feedback, and seers should learn to wait for the leadership to make decisions.

EXERCISES

A. Can you handle your revelations in a manner beneficial to yourself and the local church?

Discussion

____

____

____

B. Are you ready to seriously conform your lifestyle to receive revelations and tell people what God is communicating?

Discussion

C. Do you have the strength to proceed considering all of the aspects of your special gift?

Discussion

The Importance of a Personal Relationship with God

POINTS TO NOTE

1. The enhanced ability to receive revelations positions a watchman into a spiritual place that attracts the fury of satan. Therefore, to operate in the watchman's anointing without a personal relationship with the Triune God allows the kingdom of darkness to hijack the outworking of the giftedness for ungodly purposes. *A personal relationship with God in the operation of the watchman's anointing cannot be overemphasized.*

2. As this training manual comes to a close, let's examine the lives of two remarkable men, both of whom were remarkably gifted in the seer's and watchman's anointing. One described himself as the "Hebrew of Hebrews," and the other is a Gentile king who once ruled the most powerful and occult nation of his generation—Paul and King Nebuchadnezzar.

   Paul said of himself, *"circumcised on the eighth day, of the people of Israel, of the tribe of Benjamin, a Hebrew of Hebrews; in regard to the law, a Pharisee; as for zeal, persecuting the church; as for righteousness based on the law, faultless"* (Phil. 3:5-6). Paul was a highly gifted man who pursued the law with intense passion. After his dramatic encounter with the Lord Jesus Christ, he received incredible amounts of revelation from the throne of God, which resulted in his writing most of the New Testament—an outstanding watchman to the Body of Christ.

   The other man was King Nebuchadnezzar, who also received revelation by pictures and other forms of visual revelation. He was the head of the most occult group operating during that time. Despite being in the midst of occult practices, he had many notable dreams and visions from God, even acknowledging the supremacy of the Hebrew's God. Unfortunately, his gifting was never consecrated to God and is an example of a wasted anointing.

As the Bible says, *"Every good and perfect gift is from above, coming down from the Father of the heavenly lights, who does not change like shifting shadows"* (James 1:17).

3. Unless the Lord gives divine revelations, no one can receive them. Unfortunately, many gifted people today are operating outside the Kingdom of God. In most instances, these gifted people do not know the Triune God and inadvertently operate with power from the dark side. Without God, the seer giftedness is restricted to operating only in information shifting, because *divine revelation comes only from God.* The devil cannot tell the future. Any giftedness operating without the fruit of the Holy Spirit can be perverted.

   The Bible introduced Paul, then known as Saul of Tarsus, as a remarkable young man and one of the most zealous Pharisees of his days:

   > *At this they covered their ears and, yelling at the top of their voices; they all rushed at him* [Stephen], *dragged him out of the city and began to stone him. Meanwhile, the witnesses laid their coats at the feet of a* ***young man named Saul****. While they were stoning him, Stephen prayed, "Lord Jesus, receive my spirit." Then he fell on his knees and cried out, "Lord, do not hold this sin against them." When he had said this, he fell asleep* (Acts 7:57-60).

   Apostle Paul later confirmed this: *"I was advancing in Judaism beyond many my own age among my people and was extremely zealous for the traditions of my fathers. But when God who set me apart from my mother's womb and called me by his grace, was pleased to reveal his son in me so that I might preach him among the Gentiles, my immediate response was not to consult any human being"* (Gal. 1:14-16).

   Paul's conversion from Judaism to Christianity gives a fascinating scriptural episode:

   > *Meanwhile, Saul was* ***still breathing out murderous threats against the Lord's disciples****. He went to the high priest and asked him for letters to the synagogues in Damascus, so that if he found any there who belonged to the Way, whether men or women, he might take them a prisoners to Jerusalem. As he neared Damascus on his journey, suddenly as light from heaven flashed around him. He fell to the ground and heard a voice say to him, "Saul, Saul, why do you persecute me?" "Who are you, Lord?" Saul asked. "I am Jesus, whom you are persecuting," He replied. "Now get up and go into the city, and you will be told what you must do." The men traveling with Saul stood there speechless; they heard the wound but did not see anyone. Saul got up from the ground, but when he opened his eyes he could see nothing. So they led him by the hand into Damascus. For three days he was blind, and did not eat or drink anything. In Damascus there was a disciple named Ananias. The Lord called to him in a vision, "Ananias!" "Yes, Lord," he answered. The Lord told him, "Go to the house of Judas on Straight Street and ask for a man from Tarsus named Saul, for he is praying. In a vision he has seen a man named Ananias come and place his hands on him to restore his sight"* (Acts 9:1-12).

   Paul later wrote about the knowledge of Christ as all-surpassing:

   > *But whatever were gains to me I now consider loss for the sake of Christ. What is more, I consider everything a loss because of* ***the surpassing worth of knowing Christ Jesus my Lord, for whose sake I have lost all things****. I consider them garbage, that I may gain Christ and be found in*

> *him, not having a righteousness of my own that comes from the law, but that which is through faith in Christ—the righteousness that comes from God on the basis of faith. I want to know Christ—yes, to know the power of his resurrection and participation in his sufferings, becoming like him in his death, and so, somehow, attaining to the resurrection from the dead* (Philippians 3:7-11).

On the other hand, King Nebuchadnezzar's ability to spiritually see in the book of Daniel had a profound revelation regarding the future of his kingdom. However, Nebuchadnezzar had no right standing with God, coupled with the busyness that rulership demanded of him, so he could not remember his dream. It simply became unfruitful to him, even though the gift or the potential to receive revelations remained in his life. The misplaced urge to seek a meaning for his dream drove him to excessive compulsion causing him to threaten to kill his wise men. This gifted man suffered perversion of his gifting that was eventually frustrated by God.

EXERCISES

A. How do you relate to these two men: Apostle Paul and King Nebuchadnezzar?

Discussion

B. How can you become more like the apostle Paul?

Discussion

C. Without God, your giftedness becomes restricted to operating only in information shifting. Any giftedness operating without the fruit of the Holy Spirit will, in time, become perverted and eventually frustrated by God. Do you believe this?

Discussion

PRACTICAL PRINCIPLES AND DISCUSSION

Conclusion

In conclusion, I turn again to one of the greatest watchmen in the Body of Christ—the apostle Paul. Writing from his lonely jail cell, Paul reflects on life and writes in the first epistle to the Thessalonians words of edification, exhortation, and comforting in more than five places:

> *For our exhortation did not come from error or uncleanness nor was it in deceit* (1 Thessalonians 2:3 NKJV).
>
> *As you know how we exhorted, and comforted, and charged every one of you as a father does his own children* (1 Thessalonians 2:11 NKJV).
>
> *Therefore comfort one another with these words* (1 Thessalonians 4:18 NKJV).
>
> *Therefore comfort each other and edify one another just as you also are doing* (1 Thessalonians 5:11 NKJV).
>
> *Now we exhort you brethren, warn those who are unruly, comfort the fainthearted, uphold the weak, be patient with all* (1 Thessalonians 5:14 NKJV).

The apostle Paul stressed the importance of edification, exhortation, and comforting because as a watchman, he foresaw danger looming over the Thessalonians: *"...lest by some means the tempter had tempted you, and our labor might be in vain"* (1 Thess. 3:5 NKJV).

Edification, exhortation, and comforting are some of the pillars of an effective watchman ministry. Unfortunately, the watchman anointing has been narrowed to a "warn-them ministry" without the other essential features. We must realize the full power of this valuable ministry and bring it to its crucial relevance in this century. The 21st century watchman ministries need to widen their perspectives. The conservative, narrow, and restricted perspective of the watchman's ministry needs to accept the reality of its potential, value, and vision.

Edification

Edification identifies, by revelation, a weakness and helps build up that area; it is a basic rule of life for corporate church existence. There is a twofold expression of this process. First, to see into the supernatural sphere and prophetically identify any area in a person or group or in an institution that is weak. Second, to help strengthen that area.

Edification involves the following steps:

1. Identification of the weak area—either spontaneously revealed by God or by the prophet intentionally asking God to reveal the area.
2. Asking God to give His divine instruction and details of the nature of the weakness.
3. Determining the nature of God that would be opposite to the weakness identified.
4. Asking God for Scripture that strengthens the person, group, or church. Usually limit it to one or two prayers to allow maximum impact.
5. Praying that God would give follow-up instructions to nurture the person, group, or church in that area of weakness after the initial building up.

6. Prayerfully considering the level of elevation that God wants the person, group, or church to attain after strengthening or restoration (see Isaiah 41:8-15).

Exhortation

Exhortation turns people toward God and a place where the power of God is deliberately celebrated rather than paying undue attention to the magnitude of the onslaught of the enemy. The Bible is full of examples of this principle in action. The prophet Ezekiel, the watchman of Israel, used exhortation at a critical moment in the history of Israel:

> *This is what the Sovereign Lord says: "The enemy said of you, 'Aha! The ancient heights have become our possession.' But you, mountains of Israel, will produce branches and fruit for my people Israel, for they will soon come home. I am concerned for you and will look on you with favor; you will be plowed and sown, and I will cause many people to live on you—yes, all of Israel. The towns will be inhabited and the ruins rebuilt"* (Ezekiel 36:2,8-10).

There are various aspects of exhortation including commendation, persuasion and admonishment. Commend people to God by entreating them, using terms such as "I urge you," "I entreat you," and "I encourage you" (see Rom. 12:1-2; Phil. 4:2-3; 2 Cor. 10:1-5).

Consistently persuade people to see things from God's perspectives and if necessary repeat the prophetic promise. Admonishment calls people to a place of righteousness or a place where God wants them to be. Admonishment warns people to move away from stagnation and toward a fresh relationship with God. *Admonishing should be followed by inspiration so that stimulation or motivation can occur.*

Exhortation creates an impetus for motivation, which is exemplified by Peter in the book of Acts:

> *"Therefore let all Israel be assured of this: God has made this Jesus, whom you crucified, both Lord and Messiah." When the people heard this, they were cut to the heart and said to Peter and the other apostles, "Brothers, what shall we do?" Peter replied, "Repent and be baptized, every one of you, in the name of Jesus Christ for the forgiveness of your sins. And you will receive the gift of the Holy Spirit. The promise is for you and your children and for all who are far off—for all whom the Lord our God will call." With many other words he warned them; and he pleaded with them, "Save yourselves from this corrupt generation." Those who accepted his message were baptized, and about three thousand were added to their number that day* (Acts 2:36-41).

In addition to edification and exhortation, the watchman should know how to bring people to a place of comfort and peace in times of trouble.

Comfort

Comforting is about calming people down so they can retreat into the spirit to find peace and obtain divine strategy to face the challenges (see Ezek. 36:6-13).

Key steps in comforting:

- Distributing a measure of peace to the people.
- Enabling them to avoid worrying.
- Encouraging them to practice calmness in the midst of trouble.
- Teaching them to have absolute dependency on the majesty of God.
- Strengthening them to reinforce the power of God.
- Praying them into a place of security in God.

The prophet Jahaziel comforted Israel during a time of utter despair and hopelessness. He saw beyond the prevailing circumstance and into the spirit realm. There he saw the arm of Lord, the God of their salvation, fighting their battle:

> *All the men of Judah, with their wives and children and little ones, stood there before the Lord. Then the Spirit of the Lord came upon Jahaziel son of Zechariah, the son of Benaiah, the son of Jeiel, the son of Mattaniah, a Levite and descendant of Asaph, as he stood in the assembly. He said: "Listen, King Jehoshaphat and all who live in Judah and Jerusalem!* ***This is what the Lord says to you: 'Do not be afraid or discouraged because of this vast army. For the battle is not yours, but God's.*** *Tomorrow march down against them. They will be climbing up by the Pass of Ziz, and you will find them at the end of the gorge in the Desert of Jeruel. You will not have to fight this battle. Take up your positions; stand firm and see the deliverance the Lord will give you, O Judah and Jerusalem. Do not be afraid; do not be discouraged. Go out to face them tomorrow, and the Lord will be with you.'" Jehoshaphat bowed with his face to the ground, and all the people of Judah and Jerusalem fell down in worship before the Lord* (2 Chronicles 20:13-18).

Apostle Paul wrote: *"Rejoice in the Lord always. I will say it again: Rejoice! Let your gentleness be evident to all. The Lord is near.* ***Do not be anxious about anything, but in everything, by prayer and petition, with thanksgiving, present your requests to God. And the peace of God, which transcends all understanding, will guard your hearts and your minds in Christ Jesus.*** *Finally, brothers and sisters, whatever is true, whatever is noble, whatever is right, whatever is pure, whatever is lovely, whatever is admirable—if anything is excellent or praiseworthy—think about such things. Whatever you have learned or received or heard from me, or seen in me—put it into practice. And the God of peace will be with you* (Phil. 4:4-9). These words are comforting in whatever circumstance you may find yourself.

When a watchman operates these pivotal components, the ministry will shift from a predominantly warn-them ministry to its full potential in Christ Jesus.

I hope as you have read this section of the training manual that you now know who you really are as a watchman, that also you will know your nature and how to administer the grace of your giftedness, and even the kindness of the Giver of the gift in a new way. As the Bible says, *"the people who know their God shall be strong and carry out great exploits"* (Dan. 11:32 NKJV).

APPENDIX A

Types of Dreams and Visions

(Dreams and Visions Volume 1)

To understand dreams and visions more successfully, it is useful to take a look at the various types that can occur. This allows us to better judge our own interpretations and conclusions. Most dreams are symbolic, with God using metaphors for one object or person to represent another.

True and False Dreams

The Bible has two broad categories of dreams: true dreams and false dreams. A false dream is a product of the dreamer's own delusion. Scripture says that any dream God has not sent is a false, made-up story and delusion of the human mind. In the book of Jeremiah, God says, "I did not send them" and "their made-up dreams are flagrant lies." Consequently, you cannot receive a dream as true unless it is sent by God. If God has sent the dream, then it is a true dream with a message from Him.

Visions

A vision is a visual perception of revelation or supernatural occurrence with the spiritual eyes. A person can receive a vision even when the mind is awake. Great interplay exists between the natural and the supernatural, often with varying degrees of bodily activities and involvement of the physical realm. These bodily activities can sometimes result in healing, physical tiredness, or even physical afflictions after a visionary encounter. Most times visions need little interpretation, but they do require careful proclamation and application. They speak not only of God's nature, but also offer remarkable impartation to recipients.

Open Visions

Open visions occur when you watch an open scene with your eyes open, yet you "see" the scene in the spirit.

> *I, Daniel, was the only one who saw the vision; those who were with me did not see it, but such terror overwhelmed them that they fled and hid themselves. So I was left alone, gazing at this great vision; I had no strength left, my face turned deathly pale and I was helpless. Then I heard him speaking, and as I listened to him, I fell into a deep sleep, my face to the ground. A hand touched me and set me trembling on my hands and knees* (Daniel 10:7-10).

Divine Sight

Divine Sight is an open vision in which the natural surroundings blend into the overall scene. With divine sight, you cannot tell if the image is real or spiritual.

> *Now Moses was tending the flock of Jethro his father-in-law, the priest of Midian, and he led the flock to the far side of the wilderness and came to Horeb, the mountain of God. There the angel of the Lord appeared to him in flames of fire from within a bush. Moses saw that though the bush was on fire it did not burn up. So Moses thought, "I will go over and see this strange sight—why the bush does not burn up." When the Lord saw that he had gone over to look, God called to him from within the bush, "Moses! Moses!" And Moses said, "Here I am." "Do not come any closer," God said. "Take off your sandals, for the place where you are standing is holy ground." Then he said, "I am the God of your father, the God of Abraham, the God of Isaac and the God of Jacob." At this, Moses hid his face, because he was afraid to look at God* (Exodus 3:1-6).

Closed Visions

There are two specific types of closed visions. With your eyes closed, the image of the vision is "seen" in your mind as either:

1. Pictorial or static vision.
2. Panoramic vision (like a movie) in which there is motion.

Interactive Dreams and Visions

Interactive dreams or visions occur when an exchange happens between the dreamer and God in the encounter. For interaction to take place, the dreamer must be able to retain some degree of appropriate consciousness of his or her true, natural situation while in the dream or vision.

Interactive Visions

It seems that interactive visions are more common than interactive dreams, but your experience may be different. Perhaps this is because visions involve varying degrees of the natural realm; therefore, it is easier to retain the degree of natural consciousness required for interaction to occur in visionary encounters. Peter had an interactive vision in Acts 10:9-20 in which God unfolded His plan of salvation to the Gentiles. Another example occurs when God appeared to Ananias and commanded him to lay hands on Saul to restore his sight (see Acts 9:19-16).

Interactive Dreams

The frequency of interactive dreams reflects the glory of God available to society and the grace of God in the dreamer's life when the encounter occurs. The Lord warned King Abimelek of Sarah's true nature as Abraham's wife as a means of giving him grace from Abraham's deception in disguising their true relationship (see Gen. 20:1-7).

My Personal Experience

In an interactive dream, God once asked me to put Isaiah 54 into a song. I replied that He knew I was not a good singer and requested that He allow me to put only a few verses into a song. God insisted, however, that my song had to include the entire chapter. In the dream's next scene, I was heading home to inform my wife of the encounter. On the way, I met a gathering of Christians who were singing praises to God. I decided to join them and, to my surprise, they were all singing Isaiah 54. At the very moment I joined in, they were singing the second verse, which was being projected onto a big screen in the front of a hall. This is how the Scripture read: "Enlarge the place of your tent, stretch your tent curtains wide, do not hold back; lengthen your cords, strengthen your stakes." At this point, I woke up.

Twilight Dreams and Visions

Twilight dreams and visions, including trances, are received in twilight states. They come in various forms. Some are "breaking news"-type encounters; others are of a summary type; and many are trances. All of these manifestations are common to the ministry of a seer.

Breaking News Dreams and Visions

Breaking news *dreams and visions are characteristically short, sharp, and clear, and are given mainly for the purpose of guidance*. These manifestations are full of dream phrases, which give clear, unambiguous instructions or warnings; they are commonly associated with angelic messages and speak of "things that are happening" or what will happen shortly, hence the term breaking news. In the last days, God will increase His communication through various types of dreams. *But He will particularly increase the number and lucidity of dreams received in the twilight state*. God commonly uses breaking news dreams at critical periods in a dreamer's life to align him or her to God's purposes. Joseph, the earthly father of Jesus, had many such dreams in the time surrounding the Messiah's birth (see Matt. 1:20-21). God also uses breaking news dreams to break through our natural defenses to convey an urgent message. *On the whole, an increase in "breaking news spiritual encounters" of various sorts will occur in the last days*. Further examples of breaking news dreams/visions can be found in Jacob's dream (see Gen. 31:10-14), Laban's dream (see Gen. 31:24), and other dreams to Jesus' earthly father (see Matt. 2:12-13).

Summary Dreams

God uses summary dreams to recap the many dreams that may occur in a night. Summary dreams are common with high-volume dreamers or seers. These short dreams contain the main highlights of a night's spiritual encounters. I have had many of these dreams, and I tended to overlook them, but God revealed their purpose. Once I was on a church retreat and I was scheduled to speak the next morning. The night before I was scheduled to speak, however, I had many dreams that I couldn't remember. I woke up in the middle of the night and prayed about those dreams, even though I didn't remember them. As I drifted back to sleep, God told me in a dream that He was going to summarize that night's dreams for me, and that He had actually done this in the past even though I hadn't taken notice. The Lord then proceeded to give me main points of the night's encounters.

Trances

A trance is a state of partial or complete detachment from a person's physical surroundings to connect with the spirit realm. Trances are classic examples of twilight spiritual encounters. They can occur at any time and mimic the feeling of being between sleeping and being awake. Like breaking news dreams, trances are short, sharp, and clear and are usually rich in phrases and often involve angels. As in the Bible, they often speak to the person in unambiguous terms, mostly addressing imminent or ongoing issues that demand prompt action.

> *About noon the following day as they were on their journey and approaching the city, Peter went up on the roof to pray. He became hungry and wanted something to eat, and while the meal was being prepared, he fell into a trance* (Acts 10:9-10).
>
> *"When I returned to Jerusalem and was praying at the temple, I fell into a trance and saw the Lord speaking to me. 'Quick!' he said. 'Leave Jerusalem immediately, because the people here will not accept your testimony about me'"* (Acts 22:17-18).

Proclamation Dreams and Visions

In certain dreams and visions, we can become the voice of agreement for God to proclaim His plans on earth. Proclamation dreams and visions can also occur through the voice of an angel, a divine messenger, or ever God Himself. *Most proclamations speak of decreed events, so we are well-advised to take them seriously*. Once proclaimed, the event happens almost instantaneously in the spirit realm, although its natural manifestation may follow later (see Zech. 1:18-17). Another common form of proclamation is when God uses a respected spiritual leader or worldwide leader to declare an insightful spiritual statement relevant to the dreamer's life. Sometimes the dreamer makes the proclamation and declares profound insights into a situation. *On the surface, such proclamations may be totally out of context with a dream's setting, but they can be deeply relevant to certain situations in the dreamer's circumstances.*

Predictive and Corrective Dreams

Predictive dreams offer foresight. They can be:

- ***Prophetic dreams:*** Numbers 12:6; Deuteronomy 13:1-2; and First Samuel 28:6.
- ***Blessing and destiny dreams:*** Genesis 28:10-12; 37:5-11; and First Kings 3:5.
- ***Turning point dreams:*** the butler's dream in Genesis 40:9-15.

Corrective dreams are insightful and can take the following forms:

- ***Warning and correction dreams:*** Job 33:14-18; Daniel 4:4-27; Genesis 20:3; and Matthew 27:19.
- ***Encouragement and confirmation dreams:*** Judges 7:13-15.
- ***Guidance dreams:*** Acts 16:10.

Dreams/Visions that Call to Service and Commission

Certain dreams or visions can register God's call and/or commissioning to a person's divine destiny in the Lord. Two examples of this are when Saul (Paul) was brought out of his lifetime career of persecuting Christians, and when Isaiah accepted his prophetic call with the purification of his lips.

> *"Who are You, Lord?" Saul asked. "I am Jesus, whom you are persecuting," he replied. "Now get up and go into the city, and you will be told what you must do"* (Acts 9:5-6).

> *In the year that King Uzziah died, I saw the Lord, high and exalted, seated on a throne; and the train of his robe filled the temple. Above him were seraphim, each with six wings: With two wings they covered their faces, with two they covered their feet, and with two they were flying. And they were calling to one another: "Holy, holy, holy is the Lord Almighty; the whole earth is full of his glory." At the sound of their voices the doorposts and thresholds shook and the temple was filled with smoke. "Woe to me!" I cried. "I am ruined! For I am a man of unclean lips, and I live among a people of unclean lips, and my eyes have seen the King, the Lord Almighty." Then one of the seraphim flew to me with a live coal in his hand, which he had taken with tongs from the altar. With it he touched my mouth and said, "See, this has touched your lips; your guilt is taken away and your sin atoned for." Then I heard the voice of the Lord saying, "Whom shall I send? And who will go for us?" And I said, "Here am I. Send me!" He said, "Go and tell this people: 'Be ever hearing, but never understanding; be ever seeing, but never perceiving'"* (Isaiah 6:1-9).

Healing and Deliverance in Dreams

Many dreamers have received emotional healing in dreams, and testimonies of physical healing are plentiful. Several instances in Scripture depict dreamers either being strengthened physically or receiving encouragement in dreams. Some possible reasons why the dream atmosphere is conducive for such occurrences include:

- In dreams, God bypasses our logic, our preconceived notions, and other obstacles of the conscious mind to connect with our spirit, which is our center. *Perhaps, like a mirror, a dream may have most relevance when it reflects what is wrong with us. However, this can be where we misunderstand our dreams the most.*
- Dreams are where our spirit and soul return to find balance and real purpose in life, in an atmosphere not dominated by our mind.
- In our dreams and visions, God may show us where we have yet to take on a Christ-like attitude in life. See Peter's vision in Acts 10:14-16.
- God can give divine impartation in dreams to overcome our issues, problems, and fears.
- In dreams, God can take us back in time to reveal what needs to be properly dealt with.
- God can impart the required grace, mercy, and power for healing afflictions.
- A dreamer can become the voice of proclamation in a dream to decree a healing or deliverance on earth.

Emotional healing takes place in dreams or visions when (and if) we submit to it. In Acts 10:9-16, for example, God delivered the apostle Peter from the mindset that only the Jews were qualified for salvation. In terms of healing, there should be deliverance from hurts that occurred in our negative experiences, as well as from ungodly soul ties and unconfessed, habitual sins. Deliverance is also necessary from other destructive influences, including the spirits of Jezebel, divination, and witchcraft. Healing is also necessary from unforgiveness, bitterness, and a critical or judgmental spirit. Until healing occurs, the enemy has an open door to terrorize a person, and this extends to dreams as demonic activities or nightmares. When God heals the trauma, the memory is also healed and nightmares may disappear. This has been my testimony. One can say that fear damages the pictorial center and, quite possibly, also our word depository, which then plays up in our dreams as negative experiences.

Theophanic Dreams

Theophanic dreams are ones in which God appears and comes in the fullness of His glory and with awesome, reverential fear. His appearance is so powerful that the dreamer is compelled to listen. An example of a theophanic dream is when Abimelek speaks to God in Genesis 20:1-7.

Dialoguing with God in Dreams

Dialoguing with God often takes the form or a series of dreams in which the dreamer awakens between dreams and intercedes in response to the preceding dream. God then replies to the dreamer's response with another dream so as to continue the discussion.

On many occasions, I have had a dialogue with God in my dreams. I once had a series of seven dreams in about an hour, and all the dreams were on the same subject. In this encounter, God gave me progressive revelations in response to my intercession. Dialoguing in dreams can span a period of minutes, hours, days, weeks, or months. Therefore, it is most important that the dreamer record all his or her dreams.

We should ask God to give further information on anything revealed to us in dreams. Most of the time, God wants to continue speaking to us on these issues. Also, the majority of recurring dreams are God's progressive revelations on issues that the dreamer does not properly understand or has not adequately dealt with; the repetition is usually to address the dreamer's inner uncertainty or confusion.

One biblical example is found when Joseph (of the coat of many colors) had two dreams consisting of different details, yet they were on the same subject (see Gen. 37). Joseph's two dreams constituted a pair of dialoguing dreams. After the first dream, Joseph and his brothers responded to the dream. Then God continued His discourse by releasing the second dream (see Chapter 2). Also, the repetition of Joseph's dreams indicates God's emphasis on the subject.

Abraham's dream in Genesis 15 is a combination of an interactive and dialoguing dream. In this visitation, God reassures Abraham about the future promise of his descendants. This encounter includes an interactive vision (verses 1-9), an interlude (verses 10-11) and the furtherance of his discussion with God (verses 12-18).

"This Is That" Phenomenon

A seer may not instantly gain full understanding of all that he receives. And there are many reasons why this may happen. Oftentimes, God will prompt a seer to recall relevant revelations when the need arises. Observe how God dealt with Samuel in regard to Israel's future leader, Saul:

> *Now the day before Saul came, the Lord had revealed this to Samuel: "About this time tomorrow I will send you a man from the land of Benjamin. Anoint him leader over my people Israel; he will deliver my people from the hand of the Philistines. I have looked upon my people, for their cry has reached me." When Samuel caught sight of Saul, the Lord said to him, "This is the man I spoke to you about; he will govern my people"* (1 Samuel 9:15-17).

Through the "this is that" phenomenon, Jesus' disciples recalled the Old Testament writing, *"zeal for your house consumes me,"* as was previously prophesied in Psalm 69:9.

> *When it was almost time for the Jewish Passover, Jesus went up to Jerusalem. In the temple courts he found men selling cattle, sheep and doves, and others sitting at tables exchanging money. So he made a whip out of cords, and drove all from the temple courts, both sheep and cattle; he scattered the coins of the money changers and overturned their tables. To those who sold doves he said, "Get these out of here! Stop turning my Father's house into a market!" His disciples remembered that it is written: "Zeal for Your house will consume me"* (John 2:13 -17).

The following Scripture from the prophet Joel was recalled by the apostle Peter in Acts 2:15-21 as he addressed the crowd on the Day of Pentecost:

> *Even on my servants, both men and women, I will pour out my Spirit in those days. I will show wonders in the heavens and on the earth, blood and fire and billows of smoke. The sun will be turned to darkness and the moon to blood before the coming of the great and dreadful day of the Lord. And everyone who calls on the name of the Lord will be saved; for on Mount Zion and in Jerusalem there will be deliverance, as the Lord has said, even among the survivors whom the Lord calls* (Joel 2:29-32).

Most dreamers may have experienced this phenomenon without recognizing it. Commonly, many feel familiarity with a place where they have never been in the natural. Truth be told, the majority of such cases are due to a quickening of spiritual familiarity from their own spirit.

Premonitory Deep and Heavy Sleep

Some seers or watchmen are hit with a premonition of imminent, deep, heavy sleep when God wants to break through daily routines. The Lord does this to convey an urgent message in a dream, vision, or trance—because in order to receive a dream, one's mind needs to be asleep, whether it is day or night.

Over the years, I have learned to discern when this unusual sense of premonition comes upon me. I have never found it to be crippling or disabling. Actually, this sleep is quite short and pleasant, even though deep and heavy. If resisted, the urge will usually go away quite easily, but when complied with, it can lead to outstanding revelation within minutes.

Many instances of this phenomenon occur in the Bible. Most take place within the context of visionary encounters. Abraham's covenant was given in a vision, and then later concluded in a dream. Genesis 15:12 says, *"As the sun was setting, **Abram fell into a deep sleep**, and a thick and dreadful darkness came over him."* In this sleep, God revealed what Abraham's mind was unable to comprehend at the time of his dream.

Falling into Deep Sleep within a Visionary Encounter

God sends such deep sleep in order to bypass the mind, connect with the spirit, and avoid the seer's mindset. This is necessary to impress the spirit with what the mind may be incapable of comprehending at the time.

> *Then I heard him speaking, and **as I listened to him, I fell into a deep sleep**, my face to the ground* (Daniel 10:9).

> *So the man gave names to all the livestock, the birds in the sky and all the wild animals. But for Adam no suitable helper was found. **So the Lord God caused the man to fall into a deep sleep;** and while he was sleeping, he took one of the man's ribs and then closed up the place with flesh. Then the Lord God made a woman from the rib he had taken out of the man, and he brought her to the man* (Genesis 2:20-22).

Apparitions

Apparitions are visionary manifestations of the supernatural in the physical realm and perceived by natural senses. Apparitions were very common in biblical days. Although still quite common in modern times, many people experience them without realizing it. An apparition can be a tangible experience or an actual happening of a supernatural event in the physical realm.

Sometimes, they are barely more than mere sight; and at other times, they are a tangible sense of an actual experience in the physical realm. Apparitions are an example of interplay between spiritual and natural in visionary encounters. Most of them are interactive. Observe the phenomenon of apparitions in the following Bible passages:

> *King Belshazzar gave a great banquet for a thousand of his nobles and drank wine with them. While Belshazzar was drinking his wine, he gave orders to bring in the gold and silver goblets that Nebuchadnezzar his father had taken from the temple in Jerusalem, so that the king and his nobles, his wives and his concubines might drink from them. So they brought in the gold goblets that had been taken from the temple of God in Jerusalem, and the king and his nobles, his wives and his concubines drank from them. As they drank the wine, they praised the gods of gold and silver, of bronze, iron, wood and stone. Suddenly the fingers of a human hand appeared and wrote on the plaster of the wall, near the lampstand in the royal palace. The king watched the hand as it wrote. His face turned pale and he was so frightened that his legs became weak and his knees were knocking* (Daniel 5:1-6).

> *That night Jacob got up and took his two wives, his two female servants and his eleven sons and crossed the ford of the Jabbok. After he had sent them across the stream, he sent over all his possessions. So Jacob was left alone, and a man wrestled with him till daybreak. When the man saw that he could not overpower him, he touched the socket of Jacob's hip so that his hip was wrenched as he wrestled with the man. Then the man said, "Let me go, for it is daybreak"* (Genesis 32:22-26).

After six days Jesus took with him Peter, James and John the brother of James, and led them up a high mountain by themselves. There he was transfigured before them. His face shone like the sun, and his clothes became as white as the light. Just then there appeared before them Moses and Elijah, talking with Jesus. Peter said to Jesus, "Lord, it is good for us to be here. If you wish, I will put up three shelters—one for you, one for Moses and one for Elijah." While he was still speaking, a bright cloud covered them, and a voice from the cloud said, "This is my Son, whom I love; with him I am well pleased. Listen to him!" When the disciples heard this, they fell facedown to the ground, terrified. But Jesus came and touched them. "Get up," he said. "Don't be afraid." When they looked up, they saw no one except Jesus (Matthew 17:1-8).

When they had crossed, Elijah said to Elisha, "Tell me, what can I do for you before I am taken from you?" "Let me inherit a double portion of your spirit," Elisha replied. "You have asked a difficult thing," Elijah said, "yet if you see me when I am taken from you, it will be yours—otherwise, it will not." As they were walking along and talking together, suddenly a chariot of fire and horses of fire appeared and separated the two of them, and Elijah went up to heaven in a whirlwind. Elisha saw this and cried out, "My father! My father! The chariots and horsemen of Israel!" And Elisha saw him no more. Then he took hold of his garment and tore it in two (2 Kings 2:9-12).

Now when Joshua was near Jericho, he looked up and saw a man standing in front of him with a drawn sword in his hand. Joshua went up to him and asked, "Are you for us or for our enemies?" "Neither," he replied, "but as commander of the army of the Lord I have now come." Then Joshua fell facedown to the ground in reverence, and asked him, "What message does my Lord have for his servant?" The commander of the Lord's army replied, "Take off your sandals, for the place where you are standing is holy." And Joshua did so (Joshua 5:13-15).

APPENDIX B

The Principles of Active Waiting

(Dreams and Visions Volume 1)

Waiting does not imply not doing something about the revelation. Rather, it means actively waiting with expectation, while pondering and remaining sensitive in spirit. The principles of active waiting are well-enunciated by the prophet Habakkuk regarding what God told him concerning his complaints:

> *I will climb my watchtower now and wait to see what answer God will give to my complaint. And the Lord said to me: "Write my answer on a billboard, large and clear, so that anyone can read it at a glance and rush to tell the others. But these things I plan won't happen right away. Slowly, steadily, surely the time approaches when the vision will be fulfilled. If it seems slow, do not despair, for these things will surely come to pass. Just be patient! They will not be overdue a single day!"* (Habakkuk 2:1-3 TLB)

The following points stand out from the passage:

- The need for prayers: ***"climb my watchtower."***
- It is your responsibility to take some form of action on your revelation: Write it ***"on a billboard."***
- Seek clear understandings of your dream/vision in order to understand and prioritize your response: ***"large and clear."***
- Wait for it; the vision is for an appointed time: ***"Just be patient."***
- Hold on to your promise: ***"Do not despair, for these things will surely come to pass."***
- Dream or vision speaks of the end—it doesn't lie.

Here are five things to remember while waiting for a dream's fulfillment:

1. Do not force the situation.
2. Fulfillment belongs to God. He is more than able to fulfill what He has promised.
3. Do not be weary in doing what is right.
4. Do not neglect fellowship with God. Human counseling is essential, but divine guidance in the form of direct witness from God is even more important.
5. Do not use your personal circumstance to determine the feasibility of the promise.

APPENDIX C

Life Application and Appropriation of Dreams

(Dreams and Visions Volume 1)

When implementing this information to your life:

1. Only confirmed, correctly interpreted dreams should be applied.
2. Apply the dream and its symbols to yourself.
3. Start with simple changes that do not entail major shifts in your circumstances, unless the dream specifically says to do so.
4. Always move according to the proportion of your faith; without faith, it is impossible to please God.
5. Appropriate the dream.

   Appropriation is the process by which the dreamer in faith assumes or adopts the promise of the dream. Appropriation consists of:

   - Faith.
   - Diligent seeking, such as studying relevant Bible passages.
   - Preparing the soil of your heart by encouraging yourself in the Lord.
   - Paying attention to fine details.

APPENDIX D

Partial Dictionary of Prophetic Symbols

(The Watchman)

A

Acid: something that eats from within; keeping offense, hatred, or malice.

Adultery: unfaithfulness, either in the spirit or in the natural; actual adultery.

Airport: a ministry that sends out missionaries; a high-powered spiritual church capable of equipping and sending out ministries; preparation for ministry/provision, or nourishment in readiness for service.

Alligator: a large-mouthed enemy; verbal attacks.

Altar: a place set apart for spiritual rituals or prayers/worship, whether good or bad.

Anchor: the pillar that an object or person hangs on, or builds hope upon.

Ankles: little faith; early stages.

Anoint: equipping with the Holy Spirit for service; the power of Holy Spirit to do a work; sanctification to be set apart.

Ant: industrious; ability to plan ahead; conscious of seasons of life; unwanted guest.

Ark: an object of strength; relating to God's presence.

Arm: power and strength, whether good or bad.

Armies: spiritual warriors, whether good or bad.

Arrows: powerful words, whether good or bad; Word of God; curses from the devil; spiritual children; good or bad intentions.

Ashes: signs of repentance or sorrow.

Attic: the mind zone; a thought process; the spirit realm; memories/past issues/stored up materials.

Autograph: prominence or fame.

Autumn: transition; end of one phase and beginning of another.

Axe: the Word of God; to encourage by kind words; issues that need to be settled.

B

Baby: new Christian; the beginning of something new; beginning to be productive, something in its infancy or early stages.

Back: pertaining to the past or behind the dreamer; something concealed from view or understanding.

Backside: something in the past or behind the dreamer; something concealed from view or understanding.

Baking: making provision for feeding people; preparation for welfare ministry; God's provision.

Balances: something reflecting both sides of the matter; waiting to tilt one way or the other; judgment.

Balm: healing; anointing; something to relieve pains, stress, or agony.

Bank: heavenly account; God's favor for a future season; a place of safety and security; God's provision.

Banner (or flag): the covering to which everyone belongs or is committed to; something that brings unity, love, or purpose; a unifying object or circumstance; victory.

Banquet: God's provision; a full cup; plentiful affluence and abundance; satisfaction; blessing; celebration; structured teaching of the Word of God.

Barn: a place of provision; a church; stored spiritual wealth.

Barrenness: unproductive; a difficult time or period.

Basement: the unseen part of something; storage zone; related to the foundation; hidden.

Basket: a measure of God's provision; a measure of judgment.

Bathroom: a period of cleansing/entering a time of repentance; a place of voluntary nakedness or facing reality in individual life.

Beam: power or illumination coming from God or the heavenly; a time of exposure or spotlight.

Bear: danger; wicked person or spirit; vindictiveness; evil; something that is after what you possess.

Bedroom: a place of intimacy; a place of rest, sleep, or dreams; a place of covenant; producing sweetness.

Bees: danger; wicked person or spirit; vindictiveness; evil; something that is after what you possess.

Bells: call to attention or action; to bring to alertness; to say it loudly; public warning.

Belly: feelings; desires; spiritual well-being; sentiment.

Bicycle: a ministry depending on much human effort; a one-person ministry.

Binoculars: looking ahead; looking into the future; prophetic ministry.

Bird: symbol of leader, whether evil or good at different levels; Holy Spirit or evil spirit.

Black: lack; famine; evil; demonic spirit; darkness.

Bleeding: hurting; losing spirituality; verbal accusation; traumatic.

Blind: lack of understanding; ignorance; not able to see into the spirit world.

Blood: atonement; to appease; something that testifies.

Blood transfusion: getting new life; rescuing situation.

Blue: spiritual; Heaven-related visitation from God or the Holy Spirit.

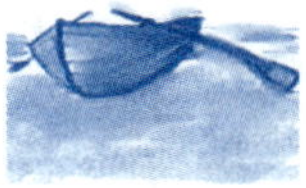

Boat: a ministry capable of influencing many people.

Body odor: unclean spirit; after-effect of fleshy actions.

Bones: the substance of something; the main issue; long lasting; (if a skeleton) something without flesh/substance, or details.

Book: gaining understanding/knowledge; Scriptures; revelation; promise from God; message from title of the book.

Bottle: relating to the body as the container of anointing.

Bow: source from which attacks come; (if an arrow) the power of a nation or person; verbal attacks; the tongue.

Bowl: a measure of something.

Bracelet: pertaining to pride; valuable, but of the world; identity, if it has a name.

Breast: source of milk for new Christians; source of sustenance; an object of enticement.

Breastplate: God's protective shield; protective of vital issues.

Bride: the Church's relationship to Jesus; special to Jesus; covenant or relationship.

Bridge: something that takes you across an obstacle, such as faith; a connection between two objects or circumstances; something that holds you up in times of difficulty.

Bridle: put control over, such as self-control over using the tongue; something imposed by a higher authority to affect control, for either good or bad.

Brook: provision of God; something that brings refreshment; wisdom; prosperity from God; if dirty, it means corrupted or contaminated.

Broom: in the process of getting rid of sins; a symbol of witchcraft.

Brother: a Christian brother or sister (spiritual brother); your own brother, or someone with similar qualities.

Building: symbolic of spiritual and emotional being of a place, person, or church; life of a person, church, or office.

Butter: encouragement; something that brings soothing, smooth words.

C

Cake: provision from Heaven.

Candle: Word of God.

Lamp or electricity: Word of God; symbolic of humankind's spirit; a lack of God's presence when unlit; conscience.

Candlestick: people who carry the light of God; the lampstand; Spirit of God; the Church.

Carpenter: Jesus; someone who makes or amends things.

Cat: a deceptive situation/person; unclean spirit; craftiness; witchcraft waiting to attack; a precious habit that could be dangerous; a personal pet.

Cave: safe hiding place; a secret place of encountering God.

Chain: symbolic of bondage or captivity; to be bound in the spirit or in the natural.

Chair: authority over something; coming to position of authority; throne of God.

Cheetah: unclean spirit.

Chicken: an evangelist; gifting; caring spirit; gathering.

Circle (ring or round): a circumstance that is endless and signifies agreement or covenant; hunting, if making a circle; relating to the universe.

Circumcision: cutting off fleshly things; coming to liberty; covenanting with God; blood relationship; new levels of spiritual walk; born again.

City: the makeup of a person; all that has been input in a person or people; group; church.

Classroom: a time of spiritual preparation; a person with a gifting to teach others.

Clay: delicate and fragile; not secure; something that refers to frailty of humanity.

Clock: timing is important in the situation; time to do something revealed; an actual time may refer to Bible passages; running out of time.

Closet: hidden, confidential, personal, or exclusive; a place of prayer.

Clothing: covering, whether pure or impure; your standing or authority in a situation.

Tearing clothes: covering; God is providing; grief and sorrow.

Clouds: heavenly manifestation; glory of God's presence; a dark time or travel; fear, trouble, or storms of life.

Dark Clouds: a stormy time.

White Clouds: glory of God.

Clown: not a serious person; not taking God seriously; childish.

Coat: mantle; protective covering; righteousness (if clean); not righteous or unclean (if dirty).

College: promotion in the Spirit.

Columns: a spirit of control and manipulation.

Cord: enhancing unity/love; something that holds things together, such as a three-fold cord.

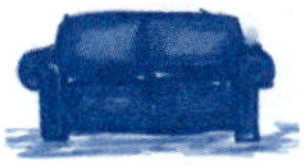

Couch: rest and relaxation; peace.

Countryside: a time of peace/tranquility; a potential that is not yet explored.

Courthouse: a time of being judged or persecution.

Cow: food/source of enrichment; a potential source of sin.

Crawling: humility or to be humiliated.

Crooked: distorted; not straight.

Crossing street: changing perspective.

Crown: symbol of authority; seal of power; Jesus Christ; to reign; to be honored.

Crying: actual crying; a period of grief; outburst of sadness; intense emotional expression.

Cultural clothes: call to a nation.

Contact Information

For additional copies of this training manual and other products from Cross House Books, contact: sales@crosshousebooks.co.uk.

Please visit our Website for product updates and news at www.crosshousebooks.co.uk.

Other Inquiries

CROSS HOUSE BOOKS
Christian Book Publishers
245 Midstocket Road, Aberdeen, AB15 5PH, UK

info@crosshousebooks.co.uk
publisher@crosshousebooks.co.uk

"The entrance of Your Word brings light."

Ministry and Contact Information

THE FATHER'S HOUSE
Spreading the love of the Father abroad

The Father's House is a family church and a vibrant community of Christians located in Aberdeen, Scotland, United Kingdom. The Father's House builds bridges of hope across generations, racial divides, and gender biases through the ministry of the Word.

You are invited to come and worship if you are in the area.

For location, please visit the church's Website:
www.the-fathers-house.org.uk

For inquiries:

Email: info@the-fathers-house.org.uk
Call: 44 1224 701343

New Titles from
Cross House Books

Times of Refreshing Volume 2

Times of Refreshing Volume 2 gives readers the ability to tap in to daily supernatural experiences! As with *Times of Refreshing Volume 1*, Volume 2 overflows with inspiring messages, comforting prayers, and Scriptures that bring His presence home. These daily boosts of God's love are just what the Divine Doctor ordered for a healthy mind, body, and spirit. Each page includes a Scripture and God-given message, as well as space for interactive exchanges of the reader's written word with His. An added bonus is a listing of Scriptures to read the Bible in a year. Prophetic Prayer Points conclude this volume of encouraging and motivating messages of daily living the supernatural, victorious life in God's Kingdom.

Growing God's Kingdom

Written by an experienced Bible scholar and beloved pastor, the insights and depth of God's word is thoughtfully shared so that newborn Christians and mature believers alike can understand and appreciate. Prefaced with an intriguing prophecy, *Growing God's Kingdom* contains practical principles that reveal the importance of God's mandate to share the gospel. You will learn about being mentored and mentoring those next in line to inherit God's riches.

40 Names of the Holy Spirit

The names of God represent a deliberate *invitation to you* to take advantage of what God can and wants to be in your life. Whatever you call Him is what He will become to you. Do you know all of His names? How much deeper would you like to know the Comforter? You will learn: Seven Symbols of the Holy Spirit; Names of the Holy Spirit; Seven Things *Not* to Do to the Holy Spirit; Twentyfold Relationship with the Holy Spirit; Fourfold Presence of the Holy Spirit; Seven Keys to Receiving the Holy Spirit Baptism—and much more!

Destined for the Top

Destined for the Top presents simple and proven successful answers to life's most complex questions. Divided into two parts—Life Issues and Family Issues—you can be at the top of your game in every aspect of your life by knowing what and who to avoid during your journey to the top. Through an added feature of thought-provoking questions at the end of each chapter, you will learn how to strengthen your spirit, invest in your potential, and realize how fickle your feelings really are. You will discover how God's wisdom and love through you propels you toward fulfilling your destiny!

Books by Dr. Joe Ibojie

How to Live the Supernatural Life in the Here and Now—BEST SELLER

Are you ready to stop living an ordinary life? You were meant to live a supernatural life! God intends us to experience His power every day! In *How to Live the Supernatural Life in the Here and Now* you will learn how to bring the supernatural power of God into everyday living. Finding the proper balance for your life allows you to step into the supernatural and to move in power and authority over everything around you. Dr. Joe Ibojie, an experienced pastor and prolific writer, provides practical steps and instruction that will help you live a life of spiritual harmony.

Dreams and Visions Volume 1—BEST SELLER

Dreams and Visions presents sound scriptural principles and practical instructions to help you understand dreams and visions. The book provides readers with the necessary understanding to approach dreams and visions by the Holy Spirit through biblical illustrations, understanding of the meaning of dreams and prophetic symbolism, and by exploring the art of dream interpretation according to ancient methods of the Bible.

Dreams and Visions Volume 2—NEW

God speaks to you through dreams and visions. Do you want to know the meaning of your dreams? Do you want to know what He is telling and showing you? Now you can know! *Dreams and Visions Volume 2* is packed full of exciting and Bible-guided ways to discover the meaning of your God-inspired, dreamy nighttime adventures and your wide-awake supernatural experiences!

Illustrated Bible-Based Dictionary of Dream Symbols—BEST SELLER

Illustrated Bible-Based Dictionary of Dream Symbols is much more than a book of dream symbols. This book is a treasure chest, loaded down with revelation and the hidden mysteries of God that have been waiting since before the foundation of the earth to be uncovered. Whether you use this book to assist in interpreting your dreams or as an additional resource for your study of the Word of God, you will find it a welcome companion.

The Final Frontiers—Countdown to the Final Showdown

The Final Frontiers—Countdown to the Final Showdown peers profoundly into the future. It expertly explores the emerging cosmic involvement of the seemingly docile elements of nature and their potential to completely alter the ways of warfare. Christians must not allow the things that are supposed to bless them to become instruments of judgment or punishment. *The Final Frontiers* provides you with a practical approach to the changing struggles that confront humanity now and in your future.

Times of Refreshing Volume 1

Times of Refreshing allows you to tap in to daily supernatural experiences! Overflowing with inspiring messages, comforting prayers, and Scriptures that bring His presence to you, these daily boosts of God's love are just what the Doctor ordered for a healthy mind, body, and spirit. Best-selling author and Pastor Bishop Joe Ibojie and Pastor Cynthia Ibojie bring 365 days of hope and refreshment into your personal space.